TRANSFORMING
HIGH SCHOOLS

TRANSFORMING HIGH SCHOOLS
A CONSTRUCTIVIST AGENDA

JOHN M. JENKINS, Ed.D.

TECHNOMIC
PUBLISHING CO., INC.
LANCASTER · BASEL

Transforming High Schools

a TECHNOMIC*publication

Published in the Western Hemisphere by
Technomic Publishing Company, Inc.
851 New Holland Avenue, Box 3535
Lancaster, Pennsylvania 17604 U.S.A.

Distributed in the Rest of the World by
Technomic Publishing AG
Missionsstrasse 44
CH-4055 Basel, Switzerland

Printed in the United States of America
10 9 8 7 6 5 4 3 2 1

Main entry under title:
  Transforming High Schools: A Constructivist Agenda

A Technomic Publishing Company book
Bibliography: p. 151
Includes index p. 157

Library of Congress Catalog Card No. 95-61946
ISBN No. 1-56676-378-9

CONTENTS

PART FOUR: THE LEARNING ENVIRONMENT

ACKNOWLEDGEMENTS

MANY PEOPLE HAVE influenced the writing of this book. I am indebted to the wisdom of the late Dr. J. Lloyd Trump who taught me that school change must be total to be effective. He advised that simply tinkering with the enterprise brought inconsistent results. He understood the application of field theory to education and management before it was fashionable. Dr. Stephen M. Corey was a great teacher. When I met him in the 1960s he was completing a distinguished career. In our brief acquaintance he helped me to see the importance of process in creating quality end products. His book on action research written in 1953 remains a classic.

I had the privilege of serving as an administrative intern with Dr. B. Frank Brown at Melbourne High School in Melbourne, Florida. This high school was one of the first nongraded secondary schools in the United States. The curriculum was organized so that all students had an opportunity to succeed. After a visit in 1963, the noted author Edgar Friedenberg remarked, "This is one of the few schools in which I have ever been where a student can survive for more than fifteen minutes."

Over the course of the last twenty-five years the writings of Dr. William Glasser have influenced my ideas for working with students and staff. I met him twenty-five years ago in Dallas, Texas, and we have been friends ever since. He understands that schooling is the business of teaching students information not teaching information to students.

I also acknowledge the professional counsel of Dr. Jim Keefe, Director of Research for NASSP, who, along with me, served as one of the principals in the NASSP Model Schools Project from 1969–1974. He is a true instructional leader. Jim's knowledge of personalized learning and learning style was critical in helping me see how to apply cognitive science to the improvement of schooling.

I am indebted to Dr. Fenwick English who gave me the opportunity to write a quarterly article for the *International Journal of Educational Reform*. Writing four articles per year on curriculum and instruction enabled me to crystallize my thinking and indirectly led to the writing of this book.

I am likewise indebted to Dr. Albert Pasqualatto of the Pitt Meadows-Maple Ridge School District in British Columbia for providing materials from the Thomas Haney Secondary Centre for use in this book.

The faculties of three schools, Miami Springs High School, Wilde Lake High School and the P. K. Yonge Developmental Research School were colleagues in the application of educational theory. Their willingness to test new approaches to teaching and learning is appreciated.

Finally, I want to thank my wife, Linda, for her continuing encouragement and her quality editing of this manuscript. As a practicing high school assistant principal she kept me focused on the real world of high school education.

IT IS THE purpose of this book to provide ideas and suggestions for changing high schools. The decision about what a high school should be like, however, is better left with the stakeholders of a particular school.

Since the publication of *A Nation at Risk* in 1982, educators, legislators, business leaders and other stakeholders have offered solutions to a perceived crisis in the nation's high schools. Longer school days, longer school years, tougher graduation requirements and world-class standards have all been offered as possible ways to ameliorate the problem. Some observers have even disputed the existence of a crisis and claim that the high schools are doing remarkably well given the circumstances they face (Berliner, 1992; Carson, Huelskamp and Woodall, 1991; Tanner, 1994).

Comparing international achievement test results is usually presented as a reason for changing or a reason for not changing high schools. On one hand the United States ranks rather low when compared to Japan, Germany and other countries in mathematics achievement. On the other hand the United States leads the world in the proportion of its population earning a bachelor's degree in all fields, especially in science and engineering. Looking at other indicators, however, may cause more concern than comfort. For example, 82 percent of the persons who inhabit the prison systems are high school dropouts. The average dropout rate in U.S. high schools is 25 percent and approaches 50 percent in most urban areas. A survey of employers, educators and parents by the Committee of Economic Development found that only 12 percent felt that high school graduates write well and only 22 percent said that they had a good mastery of mathematics (*Business Week,* 1992). A recent Harris poll found that only one-third of employers think that high school graduates show the ability to read and understand written and verbal instructions and only one-fourth say they are "capable of doing arithmetic functions." Two-thirds of the personnel directors of America's largest companies, moreover, report that they must screen more applicants than they did five years ago to find qualified candidates for job-entry positions.

The solution to our high school problem is not in reproducing someone else's remedies, but in thinking through this complex problem and adapting ideas to a local context. Several learnings appear relevant to this undertaking. New discoveries in the cognitive sciences clearly support the conclusion that individual learners are different in salient ways. They are different in their readiness to acquire knowledge; they are different in how they learn and how they like to learn.

Advances in technology can provide support for monitoring individual student learning and can offer links to information for students heretofore only imagined. Information, once the monopoly of the spoken and printed word, is now available instantaneously through the "magic" of television and computers. "E" mail is making air mail obsolete and may soon challenge the post office to change or go out of business.

Students come to high school plugged into the world. No longer are they merely passive receivers of canned information. They are active participants in creating their own meaning. If high schools are to remain a vital force in the formal education of students, then the experience the schools provide must be viewed by students as adding value to their lives. They must be helped to see a connection between what they do in schools and what they will be asked to do upon graduation from school.

Every demographic prediction for the future shows a changing school population. The minority group of today will become the majority population of the twenty-first century. Couple this change with the internal changes occurring in both minority and majority students and there is further reason for worry. During the 1940s and 1950s most, if not all, high school students worked hard in order to be recognized for their accomplishments. Today students want to be acknowledged for whom they are before they choose to work hard (Glasser, 1972).

Currently a window for change in high schools has opened. This window can be perceived as an opportunity to take some bold steps to improve our schools or as a vacuum to be filled by others. High school education appears at a crossroads. Either high school educators will implement changes to reflect several important new contingencies or will succumb to a variety of outside forces waiting to fill the vacuum.

This book is addressed to high school principals, assistant principals, teachers, curriculum specialists, counselors and other educators interested in invoking sound change at the building level. It is purposely divided into sections so that different practitioners may consult parts without reading the total volume. The theme of constructivism and constructivist thought pervades the text. *Part One* introduces the reader to constructivism and offers comparisons of a high school based on constructivism with the more familiar high school model. *Part Two* considers ways to organize the curriculum so that it connects with students' lives and interests. It discusses an approach to instruction that supports individual progress and individual differences in learning style. Additionally, this section includes a chapter on the importance of the goal of higher-order thinking for all students and presents ideas for teaching thinking across the curriculum. *Part Three* describes ways to organize high schools so that students are the key players in their own education and examines how time can best be used for student learning. A third chapter looks at ways to professionalize the role of teachers and advances some notions for adding to their responsibilities while reducing others. *Part Four* deals with the learning environment and explains how to establish school discipline where students take responsibility for correcting behavior which infringes on the rights of others. The final section, *Part Five,* summarizes the key elements in the book and shows how constructivist thinking applies to professionals as well as to students. Each chapter in sections two through four will conclude with some suggested "First Steps" for implementing the ideas presented. These First Steps will be offered as recommendations for those educators who wish to begin transforming an existing high school into a constructivist high school.

Student learning is the bottom line for considering any suggestions for restructuring high school education. How students construct meaning and make sense of their world are the most important ingredients in choosing what direction high school educators take for preparing students for the future. Effective lifelong learners take responsibility for their own learning. They are not passive responders to external events. We high school educators now have an enlarging database from which to make significant changes in what we teach, how we teach it and how we organize to teach it. It is my hope that this volume will assist with the process.

PART ONE

THE NATURE OF CONSTRUCTIVISM

CHAPTER 1

Constructivism: The Context for Change

Constructivism is a frame of reference, based on how children learn, for interpreting and organizing all classroom practice to enhance a child's ability to learn in any content area.—*Frank Betts (1994)*

WHAT IS CONSTRUCTIVISM?

CONSTRUCTIVISM OFFERS A new perspective on teaching and learning. It is based on advances in cognitive psychology. Unlike its predecessors, constructivism acknowledges the impact of unobservable events on human behavior. The brain is seen as an active participant in helping people make sense of reality; since each person is unique, each person's interpretation of reality is idiosyncratic.

The behaviorist tradition has dominated high school teaching for the past one hundred years, and despite new information to the contrary, it is still a major determinant in how high schools are managed and how students are taught. The behaviorist syllogism goes something like this:

> All behavior is observable.
> Learning results in a change of behavior.
> Therefore, learning must be observable.

In other words there is no such thing as a mental event. All events are clearly observable and since the activities of the mind are not observable, mind, as a concept, is not useful. The behaviorists reasoned that while mind may exist, it is an unnecessary construct in describing the learning process.

3

For the behaviorist, learning results when learners are taught to respond uniformly to an unchanging interpretation of reality. While reality may change in light of new discoveries, learning about reality is a matter of reinforcing correct responses and extinguishing incorrect ones. This philosophy has led to many of the practices found in our high schools—textbook teaching, similar teaching methods for all students, ability grouping, norm-referenced testing, normal distribution curves and rewards and punishment.

The constructivist views learning as an individual matter. No two learners are identical even though they may share common experiences. Their individual differences determine the meaning they assign to external events. Each learner constructs reality in terms of his or her prior knowledge, his or her values, his or her attitudes and his or her preferred ways of knowing. Mind serves as a mediator between the learner and the external reality. In reality there is no such thing as an external event. All events are a matter of individual interpretation.

The construction of meaning implies an active process within the individual. In a high school setting, it means information presented to students may not be the information that is received. When information is presented to students, it is not received exactly the same by any two learners. The fidelity of the reception depends on several extant variables resident within each learner. Learning, therefore, is described as more psychological than logical. No matter how logical the curriculum is presented, the outcomes are determined by the learner's previous knowledge, experiences, facility in processing information, learning style and level of development.

Historically constructivism can be traced to the writings of John Dewey who defended the cause for problem solving and project learning. He believed teaching students how to learn was as important as teaching them what to learn. For Dewey life itself was the context for present and future learning. Another constructivist, Jean Piaget equated the act of knowing with knowing how to make something. He described learning as adapting to the external environment. Within adaptation were two subprocesses: assimilation and accommodation. The learner assimilated familiar information into existing cognitive structures and accommodated unfamiliar information by creating new structures.

Piaget believed that children go through stages of development which influence their levels of learning. The particular stage of development affects the child's ability to respond to various forms of new information. He recommended that learning tasks be designed so that students stretch their cognitive structures but within the boundaries of their appropriate developmental levels, i.e., too small a challenge would tend to bore a learner while too big a leap would tend to make learning unintelligible.

Contemporary proponents of constructivism include Howard Gardner of Harvard University (1991) who observes that ". . . each child must construct his own forms of knowledge painstakingly over time with each tentative action or hypothesis representing his current attempt to make sense of the world" (p. 26). He posits three levels of understanding: the naive learner, the traditional student and the expert. In many cases, when their misconceptions go unchallenged, students remain at the naive level, in some cases even through university study. His remedy is an active learning environment where naive learners can interact with teachers and more sophisticated peers.

W. Edwards Deming (1986), whose management theories revolutionized Japanese manufacturing practices, described humans as cognitive beings trying to construct knowledge from experience. He maintained that 85 percent of the variation in product quality is the result of the failings of the system, not the workers. Management's task is to enlist the aid of the workers in identifying and overcoming obstacles to producing quality products. Considering teachers as managers of the instructional process leads to the conclusion that the quality of student learning is related directly to the quality of instruction; and quality in Deming's mind was determined by the desires of the customer (student). If people are intrinsically motivated as constructivism contends, then the process of instruction must help students connect school learning with success in their lives.

THE BASIC PRINCIPLES OF CONSTRUCTIVISM

Although different writers approach constructivism in slightly different ways there are some common threads which appear in all treatments of the concept. These common threads might serve as benchmarks for transforming high schools into places where all students can build upon the knowledge they bring to the school.

(1) Learning is an active process. Each learner is an active participant

in constructing meaning from external reality. Learners have different internal realities based on prior knowledge, attitudes, and values. From this internal frame of reference, they create their own interpretations of the external realities. In this sense the world can be said to be on each person, similar to music being on the radio. Their internal realities are personal and idiosyncratic.

(2) *Learning involves understanding concepts and procedures at ever increasing levels of complexity.* Learners engage new information at increasingly deeper levels of meaning. Learning is a dynamic process which involves trial and error. Errors are natural to the process and a useful part of the learning process. As learners advance in their learning, they form more accurate pictures of content and skills.

(3) *Learning is personal and unique to the individual student.* All learners are bound by their backgrounds, skills and levels of development at a particular point in time. Responses to external stimuli are not static, but particular to the student. Multiple interpretations of reality exist in any given instructional setting. Consequently, different pathways to similar ends are necessary.

(4) *Learning must be useful.* Students are more likely to see value in learning tasks which relate to real-world contexts. Content and skills learned in isolation do not engage learners. Wherever possible, teachers should create real-world environments that resemble the contexts in which the learning is presumed to be relevant or, at the least, explain to students how learning the content and skills will benefit them now or in the future.

(5) *True learning is based on intrinsic motivation.* Rewards and punishments do not motivate students to do their best. Pride in workmanship derives from tasks which the learners perceive as sensible, useful, interesting and related to improving the quality of their lives.

(6) *Evaluation of learning is broad based.* Multiple means of assessment should be employed in order to evaluate student learning. Having students reflect on the answers they give rather than the correctness of the answers helps the teacher to reconstruct the student's internal reality. Using metacognitive strategies enables the student to reflect on his/her own learning process. Evaluation of student learning should reconnect to the objectives for which the

learning was undertaken. Learning gaps can then be identified and new objectives established.

THE ROLE OF THE TEACHER

In a constructivist high school the teachers are expected to model the kind of learning that they expect from students. They show students what to do rather than tell them. Their relationship with students is one of a friend and fellow learner rather than a dispenser of information. They behave similarly to the coach who teaches from the side of the students rather than in front of them. Teachers motivate more and encourage students to ask questions. They help students select from a variety of sources of information and help them weigh conflicting data.

Teachers understand that learning is developmental and that new learnings build upon previous learnings. Their overriding aim is to help students engage knowledge in depth and to come to know their world with greater precision. Education for understanding is emphasized.

They understand that content cannot be imposed from outside any individual. The individual student makes the decision to learn or not to learn the content. Teaching, therefore, is a matter of persuading students that learning certain content is in their best interests.

The art of teaching requires the skill of knowing how much structure to provide and when. Constructivist teachers provide help in the beginning of a learning task but gradually remove help so that students can become more independent learners. They know their students well enough to judge when to offer help and when to withhold it. They also know salient information about their students so that learning sequences can be structured to optimize learning for individuals.

Students are given choices. Assignments can be completed in different ways. Varying pedagogy is offered. When teachers lack sufficient data about a student, they model data collection behavior by seeking out the information in various offices in the high school. They also request help from other professionals in the school.

Teachers reflect on teaching practice by engaging in action research either solo or with other teachers. They encourage students to share their ideas and to challenge the ideas of others respectfully. A problem solving atmosphere exists in the classroom or instructional area. Open-ended questions spark creative discourse. Students are encouraged to suggest causes for events and situations. They are asked to predict consequences of their actions.

Teachers are more interested in uncovering information than covering it. Students are given time to probe content more deeply and increase their understanding. Time is considered a variable not a constant. They realize it takes considerable time to learn something in depth.

Students are empowered to choose among assignments, to create their own contracts for learning, to work alone, in pairs or on a team and to match the learning venue with the task to be completed. What students have to say is important. The E. F. Hutton principle rules, "When students talk, teachers listen!"

CONSTRUCTIVISM AS A BASIS FOR RESTRUCTURING

If constructivism were to be used as a basis for restructuring a high school, what might occur? For one, students would be more actively engaged in the learning process. Lecturing would occupy only one place in the teacher's arsenal of instructional activities. More hands-on activities would be offered. Textbooks would serve as one source of information to support the attainment of learning objectives or as reference for students as they solve problems.

Classrooms of twenty-five to thirty students would be replaced by varying sized groupings consistent with the purposes of instruction. Locations for learning would likewise vary in accordance with the learning tasks. Information about students would be systematically collected, formatted and disseminated to teachers to use in creating appropriate learning environments. Learning style would be diagnosed.

Learning teams would move front and center so that students could interact with other students and with adults. Teachers would collaborate and often work together in teams. Students would be viewed as learners with different talents and gifts. Thinking would be taught across the curriculum.

Content and process would be treated as equals. Knowing how to learn would be a priority. The relationship between students and content would be considered dynamic and subject to change in lieu of changes in the learner and changes in the content. Improvement would be valued. Continuous feedback from students would be solicited to achieve improvement in the system.

Students would be provided differential time frames to complete work. Individual schedules would reflect the best time for individual students to undertake difficult tasks. Longer periods of time would facilitate students pursuing learning in depth.

Teachers would function both as specialists in subject fields and generalists responsible for helping students resolve academic and personal problems. They would understand as Barbara Presseisen (1990) observes that "teaching is no longer the transfer of discrete bits of knowledge, information accumulated in traditional packages and programs, presented in unchanging, universally recognized, units of print" (p. 13). Technological accessing of information would be encouraged and facilitated.

Success for all students would drive decision making and regulate the distribution of resources both human and financial. Student progress would be viewed incrementally in terms of progress towards individual and school goals. Students would have opportunities to improve their work in order to improve their grades. Self-evaluation would be encouraged and taught. How students are tested would come under scruitiny. Tests would more closely align with the purposes of instruction and include opportunities to apply knowledge in familiar and unfamiliar settings.

In the constructivist high school, the individual student becomes the primary unit of instruction. Instruction begins where learners are and moves them as deeply as their time, talent and motivation allow. Constructivism pushes a high school toward a more personalized approach to education.

A MODEL FOR PERSONALIZING EDUCATION

In 1969 the National Association of Secondary School Principals (NASSP) and the Danforth Foundation embarked on a bold venture to transform the American secondary school. Labelled the Model Schools Project or sometimes Schools of Tomorrow, each of the thirty-two secondary schools in the Project attempted to implement a variety of innovations simultaneously. These innovations included flexible scheduling, differentiated staffing, advisement, different instructional groupings, continuous progress instruction, common learnings in eight/nine disciplines for all students and team teaching. Dr. J. Lloyd Trump, the Project's director, thought that previous attempts at improving secondary schools had failed because the total environment in which an innovation was tried did not provide appropriate support for the innovation. Total change was needed.

The context for implementing these innovative strategies was one of a personalized approach to education where each student was known as a "total human being" educationally. In Trump's (1977) words, we must use "the process of continuous monitoring of each student with the procedures of diagnosis, prescription, implementation and evaluation (DPIE) in a progressive effort to help each student develop the hobby and career interests that lead to an interesting and productive life" (p. 27). Later, James W. Keefe, recently Director of Research for NASSP and a principal in the Model Schools Project, defined personalized education as tailoring the learning environment to the characteristics of individual students. Personalized education begins with the learner and builds the learning environment on learner needs and interests and societal demands (Keefe, 1989).

Keefe's elaboration of Trump's initial work includes the DPIE activities and twelve working components in Figure 1.1.

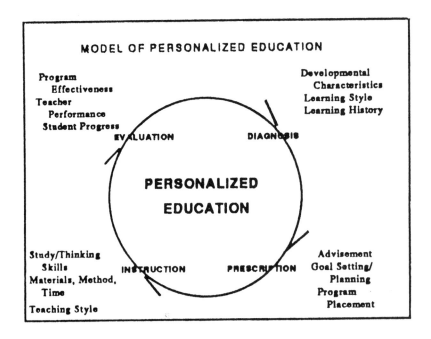

Figure 1.1. Model of Personalized Education.

Diganosis addresses student development characteristics, previous learning history and current learning style. The term diagnosis is often avoided because it seems to imply a complex task. Yet it is a familiar practice in many high schools and is implicit in such phrases as, "Her problem is . . ." and, "What he really needs is. . . ." A downside of diagnosis is when it results in the labelling of students, leading to a self-fulfilling prophecy. In the constructivist context, diagnosis would relate to the accumulated experiences and background that the learner brings to a school generally and to a particular instructional situation.

Prescription is concerned with advisement, goal setting/planning and program placement. All of these are good activities in their own right but even more effective in the total personalized model. A teacher adviser works with an individual student to translate the diagnostic information into a personalized educational plan (PEP). More will be said about advisement activities in Chapter 7.

Instruction embraces teaching style, teaching methods, time use and study and thinking skills. It is the implementation of the PEP for each student. Human variability requires that teachers consider the interactions of methodology with student characteristics, interests and use of time. Effective instruction is viewed as matching learners and appropriate instruction.

Evaluation looks at student achievement, teacher performance and program quality. It is a measure of the success of the PEP and the subsequent instruction in helping individual students to learn. Assessing student achievement in terms of anticipated outcomes enables the teacher and the student to determine the effectiveness of curriculum and instruction. If the student fails to meet the goals established in the PEP, then the plan and the instruction are revisited and revised as necessary. In some cases the discrepancy may be the result of information not included in which case the plan is also changed accordingly. The personalized model of education is dynamic. It is a continuing search for improving learning for all students.

The relevance of personalized education to constructivism seems clear. The focus is on the individual learner and incorporates individualized instruction, cooperative learning, group presentations, community-based learning experiences and independent study, all under one instructional umbrella. Appropriate learning experiences are judged in terms of helping individual learners attain school and personal goals.

CONSTRUCTIVISM AND TRADITIONAL PRACTICE

Some Final Thoughts

Table 1.1 summarizes several differences between traditional high school practices and practices that seem consistent with constructivist thought. It is the premise of this book that the practices of the past are too much with us even today. Given our present understanding of how people learn, constructivism seems a sound basis for high school reform.

In considering constructivism as a framework for high school reform one caveat seems worthy of mention. The concept of constructivism, like any concept, may mean different things to different educators. Some educators believe that since the individual creates the reality, no reality exists independent of the individual. Subject matter, therefore, is variable and illusive. Others, less radical in their interpretations, believe that there is a body of knowledge and skills worthy of teaching students, but how students approach learning is unique and different. All students cannot be taught in the same way and expect similar results. This latter position appears to make the most sense for restructuring efforts.

The bottom line for rethinking the high school, however, is student learning. All students must be helped to develop their potentials if our accustomed standard of living is to endure. Traditional high schools have failed a large portion of our school population. As the mix of students becomes more diverse, the number of minority students for whom traditional schooling has been largely ineffectual will increase. The high-stakes technologically sophisticated world in which we live requires all students to think, to problem solve, and to generate new information. The immense findings in the cognitive sciences over the past fifteen years propel us to find better ways to help students learn. The "sage on the stage" approach and the normal distribution mentality that has prevailed in the high schools for too long will not work for an increasing number of high school students.

We now have the knowledge and the technology to operate high schools differently. Today's ethos provides high school educators with a window of opportunity unlike any in the history of American education. Innovation has become an acceptable word in the public's guidebook for schools. The thrust of this change is local control. Principals

Table 1.1. Comparison of Traditional High School Practices to Practices Based on Constructivism.

Traditional	Constructivist
1. Graduation requirements are the same for all students.	Students complete similar graduation requirements with opportunities for options based on interest and goals.
2. Competition is used as a means for getting students to do their best work.	Teamwork is emphasized so that students can learn from each other.
3. Rewards, incentives and punishments motivate students to learn.	Motivation is viewed as intrinsic to the learning task for individual students.
4. Memorization of information and facts constitute much of the learning tasks.	Problem solving and the application of knowledge constitute understanding.
5. Textbooks and the teacher are the primary sources of content.	Multiple sources of information are used to help students achieve learning objectives.
6. Students are scheduled into instructional groups based on ability.	Instruction is personalized and adjusted to individual differences. Group size is dependent on the learning task.
7. The curriculum stresses the coverage of content.	The curriculum covers less content but in depth.
8. The evaluation of student progress is completed at regular intervals throughout the school year.	The evaluation of student progress is continuous. Changes in instruction are made on the basis of feedback.
9. Paper and pencil objective tests are the predominant form for assessing student learning.	Different forms of assessment are used. Open-ended questions and practical applications are common.
10. Uniform time periods are provided for classes.	Time periods are variable depending on the nature of the work to be done.

and other instructional leaders are in a unique position to influence the direction of our high schools for the better. Each is free to create his/her own meaning in reconceptualizing the American high school. Control of this process seems best in the hands of the persons closest to the learning, the student. For in the final analysis it is the student who is the entrepreneur of his/her own education.

The sections that follow offer concrete suggestions for restructuring a high school to reflect much of the constructivist perspective. The content is by no means complete. As the reader considers the suggestions in the context of his/her own background and experience, modifications of the suggestions are likely, even expected.

PART TWO

CURRICULUM AND INSTRUCTION

CHAPTER 2

Rethinking the Curriculum

Curriculum is the work plan of the school. It focuses and connects the work of teachers.—*Fenwick English (1992)*

EXCEPT FOR A brief excursion in the 1960s the high school curriculum has basically remained intact. Needless to recount, the present mathematics sequence of general mathematics—Algebra I, geometry, Algebra II, trigonometry and solid geometry has been in place since most adults were high school students. The 1960s in response to the Russian Sputnik was a time when various subject areas were awash with the development of inquiry-based curricula. Each program was identified with a particular set of initials.

You may remember mathematics was offered with SMSG (School Mathematics Study Group) or UICSM (University of Illinois Curriculum Study in Mathematics). High school science came as BSCS (Biological Sciences Curriculum Study) in four versions: blue, green, yellow and striped. Chem Study and Chem Bond were two approaches to the teaching of chemistry. Dr. Jerrold Zaccahrias of Harvard developed PSSC physics and IPI physical science. A social studies program was developed by Dr. Edwin Fenton that offered courses in world history and American history. The focus of each program was students adopting the ways of the mathematician, the historian and the scientist. In many respects all these efforts foreshadowed the advent of constructivism.

After several years, the inquiry approach was dropped largely because of complaints from the public that factual knowledge was being overlooked. The term "new math" became a synonym for confusion. Parents felt unable to help their children with homework. Higher-order thinking was eschewed in favor of recall and regurgitation. Ironically, over thirty years later, conditions have changed and once again higher-order thinking has become one of the priorities for schooling.

THE CORE COMPETENCIES

When we look at the United States today and our place in the global economy, several key skills seem necessary for success. Certainly reading and writing must be at the top of the list. All students must be able to read and to write with a high level of proficiency in order to take their place and remain in the workforce. Additionally, students need to be able to express their ideas orally in a clear and succinct manner and be able to listen to what others have to say. Consistent with the recommendations of the *Secretary's Commission on Acquiring Necessary Skills* (SCANS, 1991) report, students must likewise perform mathematical operations well. They must learn to value teamwork and cooperation. Few places in the traditional high school curriculum exist where students are taught to think on their feet. The demands of the information society require that students become competent information processors so that they can analyze the multiplicity of symbol systems which they will likely encounter in their lifetimes. They also need strategies for creating new information. Creativity can no longer be expected of only the students in the upper level courses. All students must become skilled problem solvers able to figure out what to do when they don't know what to do and able to adapt to contingencies that can only be imagined today.

Underlying these core competencies are requisite subskills and knowledge which draw from all of the disciplines. Examining the standards that have been recently developed by national professional associations can help select content and performances to support the core competencies. Combining these standards with the philosophy of constructivism can lead to a curriculum which emphasizes depth over coverage and organizes content, when possible, around problems to be solved.

THE QUEST FOR NATIONAL STANDARDS

Responding to goals three, four and five in *America 2000*, various national organizations have begun to develop standards for subject areas. Beginning in 1989 with the publication of *Curriculum and Evaluations Standards for School Mathematics*, the National Council of Teachers of Mathematics took leadership for the improvement of mathematics education in schools. This report delineated for three levels (K–4, 5–8 and 9–12) what students should know and be able to do. It set the tone for subsequent work in the areas of English, science, history and geography—all the subjects listed in goal three of *America 2000*.

The Standards Project for the English Language Arts presents standards in five strands: Reading/Literature, Writing, Language, Real-World Literacy, and Interconnections.

Science has been partially defined by two national projects—The National Committee on Science Education Standards and Assessment (NCSESA) and the American Association for the Advancement of Science (AAAS). *Science for All Americans*, a publication of AAAS, is probably the more well-known of the reports. *Project 2061*, an outgrowth of *Science for All Americans*, identifies over sixty literacy goals in science as well as mathematics, technology and the social sciences. The National Science Teachers Association (NSTA) has developed *Scope, Sequence and Coordination of Secondary School Science: The Content Core* (1993).

The History Standards Project has developed detailed standards for the teaching of history. The standards are specific and content oriented. The National Council for the Social Studies (NCSS) drafted more generalized standards for the social studies. Rather than focus on specific content, NCSS offers ten content standards formed from more generalized themes such as culture, time, continuity and change, and individual development and identity.

Like history, geography is treated as a separate discipline. Two groups have developed standards in this field, the Geography Education Writing Committee and the National Assessment of Educational Progress (NAEP). The former group structures its materials around five themes (location, place, human-environmental interaction, movement and regions). The latter translated the five instructional themes into specific outcomes for assessment.

In other works related to the social sciences and contained in goal five of *America 2000*, the Center for Civic Education has produced "National Standards for Civics and Government." They identify seventy-three content standards along with key concepts that students should know to meet the standards. Prompted by the work of all these groups, other groups are developing standards in art, foreign languages, physical education and the world of work.

The standards address K–12 education and provide a scope and sequence for helping schools and school districts organize what to teach. Most of the standards are described on a continuum with the lower levels designed for elementary school and the higher levels for the high school. The value of such an organization is that it provides an opportunity to establish a continuous flow to learning in any discipline.

SOME OPTIONS FOR THE DESIGN OF THE CURRICULUM

Using the standards work at the national level as a point of embarkation, the high school curriculum can be redefined in several ways. Jacobs (1989) recommends a continuum of options beginning with discipline-based content and ending with a fully integrated day in which students design and complete an individual project.

David Feldman (1980) offers a continuum of cognitive development. His continuum begins with a universal level, meaning that all children are expected to do these activities. At the next level, the cultural level, all persons in that particular culture can participate. At the discipline-based level, students can function within their own culture, but can also function outside the culture in certain domains. The discipline-based level is subdivided and arranged in a sequence from novice to apprentice to journeyman to craftsman to expert and, finally, to master. It is Feldman's belief that by the end of grade twelve all students should have completed the apprentice level in at least one discipline, preferably more.

Adapting Feldman's ideas to a high school would call for an identification of those learnings that would be required of all students, those learnings required of most students and those learnings which would advance students in a special area. Ostensibly, the required learnings could be discipline-based or interdisciplinary. The cultural level might focus on those learnings germane to a given school or community and again could be discipline-based or across disciplines. The separate subject levels would take students from a starting point to as far as their time, talent, and motivation enable them to go.

A way to organize curricula for high schools that I favor is to think of content in terms of three categories—Essential, Desirable and Specialized. These categories can be superimposed over the entire curriculum and stated in terms of content and/or performance objectives and applied to the content of individual subjects. The Essential content would be for all students regardless of individual bent or talent. The Desirable content would be an extension of the required learnings. Students would be strongly encouraged, but not required to pursue learning to this level. Specialized areas would enable students to create their own curricula and to work on in-depth projects alone, in pairs or in inquiry teams. Every student would be required to complete Specialized projects in the disciplines, or in some cases, a project which integrates several disciplines.

ESSENTIAL KNOWLEDGE, SKILLS AND APPLICATIONS

At the macro level requirements for graduation might be defined in terms of student competencies and expectations. Rather than a diploma signifying a collection of credits earned over four years, it could require the mastery of essential knowledge, skills and applications. The competencies might be derived by conducting a careful needs assessment which incorporated input from a variety of sources, e.g., state law, national professional organizations, the content of state mandated tests, local policy, textbooks and predictions for the future. These expectations would be required of all students and would be closely aligned with measurement tools to determine student performance that compared them with the levels of proficiency associated with the expectations. If at the end of the senior year each student was required to select an event or set of events in American history, write a library research-based paper on the effects of the event(s) on different groups of people and then to describe how the event(s) continues to affect us today, the assessment tool would naturally follow. The paper would be evaluated holistically by a panel of experts based on rubrics established by the school. Criteria for evaluating the paper would be defined in terms of competent, acceptable and unacceptable. Any student whose paper was rated acceptable or unacceptable would be given an opportunity to revise and resubmit his/her work.

Educators at Littleton High School in Littleton, Colorado have published a document which describes nineteen graduation requirements. Each requirement is accompanied by several assessment tools in which the student demonstrates competency. Figure 2.1 shows a graduation requirement, the specific skills associated with that requirement and the measurement tool for the requirement.

Scoring for judging the student's performance are described in terms

Graduation Requirement	Specific Skills	Demonstration
The L.H.S. graduate speaks and writes articulately and effectively	The student: 1) Writes using grammatically acceptable English 2) Adjusts tone and style of writing for purpose and audience 3) Supports statements using well-founded facts, theory, and opinion 4) Separates fact from opinion 5) Logically reaches conclusion based on sufficient evidence 6) Distills information 7) Clearly and succinctly states key points 8) Organizes ideas in a variety of ways 9) Demonstrates creativity through style, organization and development of content	While at L.H.S., the student accumulates 11 samples of writing assignments. These writings must include two samples from the personal, functional and creative writing types, and five from the traditional writing category. These papers are to be placed in a *Writing Portfolio* and submitted.

Figure 2.1. One of Nineteen Graduation Requirements Developed by the Staff at Littleton High School, Littleton, Colorado, 1995–1996.

of proficiency and excellence. A third level, unacceptable, is also listed. Scoring rubrics describe categories and performance levels.

The Littleton document resembles the procedures for earning merit badges from our scouting experiences. You may remember that requirements for earning a merit badge were described in a specific publication written for each of over one hundred possible merit badges. The requirements specified behaviors that the scouts must perform in order to show sufficient mastery of the behaviors for the merit badge. When the scouts were ready, they presented evidence of having met the requirements. The demonstration of proficiency was usually performed before the scoutmaster and/or others with expertise in the area. If the scouts met the standard, they were awarded a merit badge. If they did not, then they were advised about what had to be done in order to meet the standard. In the scouting system the requirements were written in a way to almost prescribe the assessment tool for measuring competency.

Figure 2.2 describes the behaviors necessary to receive a merit badge in general science.

Three more sections of requirements are provided. Two of the three require that the scouts conduct experiments, describe the scientific principles at work and report the results using appropriate scientific report writing. The scouts are encouraged to work in teams, with outside mentors or with their parents (Woodburn, 1972).

Merit badge booklets for the Boy Scouts of America may be purchased by writing Boy Scouts of America, Supply Division, National Distribution Center, 2109 Westinghouse Blvd., P.O. Box 7143, Charlotte, NC 28241-7143.

Essentials can also be described in terms of exhibitions of student work. The term Exhibition is used by Sizer (1992) to describe the prod-

---

1. Do two:
   a. Chart the movement of the moon and one planet during four hours. Relate this to a point on the horizon.
   b. Chart the position of the moon on the days or nights you can see it for one month. Sketch the shape of the moon as you see it.
   c. Chart the positions of three constellations in relation to the North Star during four hours.
   d. Watch and report on an eclipse of the moon, a meteor shower, or similar astronomical event.

2. Describe two:
   a. A streambank, a vacant lot, an area that has been recently cleared for a construction project, or some other location where erosion is taking place.
   b. An exposure of a rock stratum or strata. This can be at a road cut, an excavation, or at a natural canyon or gorge.
   c. Three different kinds of clouds and tell what atmospheric conditions existed while each kind of cloud was forming.
   d. The conditions in the environment which come immediately before and during three different kinds of precipitation.

Figure 2.2. Merit Badge Requirements for General Science, Boy Scouts of America (Woodburn, 1972).

Do the following tasks by memory:

a. Recite a poem or song that is special to your family or community.

b. Draw a map of the world, freehand (conventional Mercator projection) and be prepared to place properly on your map at least twelve of the fifteen members of the United Nations that we shall randomly draw for you.

c. Draw a map of the United States freehand and accurately position on your map at least twelve of the fifteen states that we shall select for you at random.

d. Identify and answer questions about the current United States president and vice president, this state's two United States senators, the representatives from your district, your state representatives and senator and the mayor of this city.

e. Recite from memory a speech from history or literature that you find compelling and that we agree is appropriate for this requirement.

f. Present a time line since 1750 that you have assembled over the last several years and be prepared to answer questions about any event that appeals to you.

g. Be prepared to identify five birds, insects, trees, mammals, flowers and plants from our local environment.

h. At a time mutually agreed on, we shall give you a text or an analogous "problem" (such as a machine to disassemble and reassemble) and three days in which to memorize or master it. We will then ask you to show how well you have done this task.

i. Be prepared to reflect with us on how you completed this memory task—that is, how you best "learned" to memorize.

Figure 2.3. An Example of an Exhibition Used for a Graduation Requirement (Sizer, 1992, p. 65).

ucts of a student's learning. It can be written as a series of requirements for exiting a school or a course. It says to the student when you complete running the course, this is what you are expected to exhibit. "If he does that well, he can convince himself that he can use knowledge and he can so convince others. It is the academic equivalent of being able to sink free throws in basketball" (Sizer, 1992, p. 25).

Figure 2.3 shows an Exhibition that might be used as a graduation requirement. Again, similar to the merit badge description or to the Littleton High School requirement, the assessment of the behavior seems imbedded within the task(s) itself. Students are expected to apply their knowledge and skills to specific circumstances.

Figure 2.4 presents an Exhibition written for a specific high school course in mathematics.

The Exhibition differs from the other formats for describing requirements in that its tendency is to spell out the measurement tool and imply the specific requirements. The mathematics example could have read, "the student will complete accurately a federal Internal Revenue Form 1040 and defend his/her work in a mock audit by one of his/her classmates." The Exhibition, as described, could then be used as the method for demonstrating achievement.

ORGANIZING A COURSE BY PERFORMANCE STANDARDS

Defining high school course requirements means beginning with the expectations and working backwards. Expectations for students can be written as Exhibitions, outcome indicators, content objectives or performance objectives. The important point is that they must be specific so as to enable the selection of assessment tools that are aligned with the behaviors and written unambiguously. The requirements may be ordered sequentially or nonsequentially depending on the nature of the subject matter. Units are then created for each of the requirements or

---

Your group of five classmates is to complete accurately the federal Internal Revenue Service Form 1040 for each of five families. Each member of your group will prepare the 1040 for one of the families. You may work in concert, helping one another. "Your" particular family's form must be completed by you personally, however.

Attached are completed financial records for the family assigned to you, including the return filed by that family last year. In addition, you will find a blank copy of the current 1040, including related schedules and explanatory material provided by the Internal Revenue Service.

You will have a month to complete this work. Your result will be "audited" by an outside expert and one of your classmates after you turn it in. You will have to explain the financial situation of "your" family and to defend the 1040 return for it which you have presented.

Each of you will serve as a "co-auditor" on the return filed by a student from another group. You will be asked to comment on that return.

Figure 2.4. An Example of an Exhibition Applied to a High School Mathematics Course (Sizer, 1992, p. 48).

for a grouping of requirements. Applying the Essential, Desirable and Specialized format, units are identified as fitting one of these categories. Essential units are required of all students. Desirable units will appeal to most students. Specialized units are for students who wish to pursue content in depth. In some instances students are encouraged to create their own units. In this structure all students will have an opportunity to make choices about what they are to study and at times, to participate in the design of their own curriculum.

Each unit is written so that the requirements students are to meet to receive credit are clearly spelled out. If they can demonstrate mastery of any of the requirements prior to beginning the unit, they are given credit in advance and allowed to move on. This procedure is similar to what occurs when students apply for advanced placement credit at the university. Activities for each of the requirements are varied and often allow for student choices, either independently or with the guidance of a teacher. Students are able to choose or to be assigned the activities most suitable for their interests and learning styles. In some cases the students will work in groups, in pairs or independently.

The following example is taken from a high school English course for students with modest background in reading and writing skills.

COMMUNICATIONS I   12 Units = One Credit

To the student and parent: Communications I offers a combination of teacher-directed sessions, group process experiences and supervised independent study. On the basis of test results and other observations, teachers identify student needs and design individual student programs using many options available within the course. Among these options are learning guides, reading contracts, research papers, computer assisted instruction and skills work. Students may also work in the *Skills Shop** to improve specific reading, writing or learning skills.

Every student MUST complete five required units. Four of the units will be completed in teacher-directed writing workshops. The other seven units will be selected from the available options by having students plan individually with the teacher.

**Skill shops are resource centers where students receive help one-on-one or in small groups for augmenting skill weaknesses in reading, writing or information processing.

UNITS

One. Writing workshop: This segment (and segments four, seven and ten) aims to improve student writing skills. Emphasis is placed on the development of the ability to organize logically, to use effective supporting detail and to employ proper mechanics and usage. Working independently, with a teacher and in small groups, each student will write three one-page papers each quarter. These papers will be placed in a portfolio for each student and seen as evidence of progress toward basic proficiency in writing.

Two. Learning guides: Students will work through various learning guides at their own pace. Each guide contains objectives, alternate activities and testing procedures. When students are ready to demonstrate successful completion of the objectives for a particular guide, they may request a test. The following learning guides are available: "On Writing," "Memory," "Getting Sentence Sense," "The Job Maze," "Letterwriting," "Moving Through the Media Center," "Memoir," "Profile," "Propaganda," and "The Mind's Eye."

Three. Minigroups: These groups are teacher paced and may be required of some students while offered as options for others. Offerings range from grammar instruction to various forms of literature, to dramatic activities, to instruction in information processing strategies.

Four. Writing workshop (See Segment one)

Five. Learning guides or minigroups (See Segments two and three)

Six. Open segment: An open segment is one determined jointly by the student and the teacher. It may be a learning guide, a minigroup, the skills shop or an original contract created by the student and teacher. It allows the teacher to prescribe for a student a special interest.

Seven. Writing workshop (See Segment one)

Eight. Open segment (See Segment six)

Nine. Open segment (See Segment six)

Ten. Writing workshop (See Segment one)

Eleven. Open segment (See Segment six)

Twelve. The Final Examination will assess the student's growth over the course. It will require the student to examine relationships between various segments and to demonstrate mastery of the writing skills associated with the skills practiced throughout the course.

The format of the Communications I course allows for considerable flexibility in working with students. Placement of individual students into writing workshops, minigroups, learning guides or open units is based upon a comprehensive diagnosis which includes content background, writing and reading skill levels, information processing skill levels, ability to function independently and learning style. Progress in Communications I is individual and largely in the student's control.

One caution seems necessary. The course and unit requirements are still external to individual students. How they interpret them is dependent upon the background, skills and experiences they bring to the learning and performance tasks.

There are several values inherent in this approach to designing the high school curriculum. For one, when the standards and benchmarks are clearly written, assessment seems to develop naturally, especially assessment that is more authentic than a paper and pencil test. Secondly, students can work at their own pace and not feel constrained by artificial deadlines. Thirdly, students are able to participate in designing some of their own learning sequences; and, finally, students can work on individual projects of high interest.

LEARNING GUIDES

The format for the development of learning guides is described in Chapter 5, following a schematic for organizing a course as continuous progress. An example of a learning guide for English from the Thomas Haney Secondary Centre, Maple Ridge, British Columbia follows:

INTRODUCTION

"When I use a word," Humpty Dumpty said, in a rather scornful tone, "it means just what I chose it to mean—neither more nor less." "The question is," Alice said, "whether you can make words mean so many different things." "The question is," said Humpty Dumpty, "which is to be master—that's all."

—Lewis Carroll, *Through the Looking Glass*

The purpose of this guide is to employ a new awareness of perspective to develop more effective communication skills. Recognition of what the attitudes or feelings of the people we wish to communicate with is called *awareness of audience.* In order to communicate effectively we must be aware of (1) our subject matter and (2) how our audience may react to our information.

OUTCOMES OF THIS GUIDE

Upon successful completion of this guide, you will be able to:

(*1*) Develop a better awareness of audience and use this awareness to increase communication.
(*2*) Display knowledge of format for résumés.
(*3*) Write an effective résumé using the appropriate format.
(*4*) Identify the component parts of a business letter.
(*5*) Adopt appropriate tone of language to suit the situation and audience.
(*6*) Identify point of view in prose fiction.
(*7*) Recognize advantages and disadvantages of using particular types of point of view.

EVALUATION

You will have successfully completed this guide when:

(*1*) You have attended all four seminar sessions—evaluating resumes, practical communication, literary point of view and *Flowers for Algernon.*
(*2*) You have submitted two required written assignments of average to above average quality.
(*3*) You have successfully participated in the group work associated with the seminar on *Flowers for Algernon.*
(*4*) You have logged five hours in your reading journal, verified by a teacher.

RESOURCES

You will need a loose leaf notebook, a resource list and two teacher provided textbooks: *Inside Stories II* and *Ten Top Stories.*

DIRECTIONS TO STUDENTS

Learning Activity #1

One exercise that most people need to do at one time or another is to write a *Résumé* for a job application. To do this effectively one has to anticipate what the employer is looking for in the employee (Awareness of audience) and provide him/her with information that will help one secure the job (Intent).

Like any effective communication we must first look at a format that would allow us to present the necessary information in a clear and organized fashion.
Read the following six articles in any order. They are available at the resource desk.

(*1*) *The Résumé Puts the Spotlight on You*
(*2*) *The Essential Elements of a Complete Résumé*

(3) Other Relevant Facts

(4) The Complete Letter

(5) Putting It Together Your Way

(6) The Cover Letter: It Should Be an Attention Getter

After reading the six articles make a list of the key elements to remember in making a résumé. Place this list in your notebook. Develop a résumé of yourself and arrange time to review the contents with a teacher.

Learning Activity #2

Evaluating Résumés Seminar—Sign up for one of the scheduled seminars and report on time. In this seminar you will divide into groups of three or four. The object is to assume the role of an employer. You are looking for a coordinator for an outreach program. Before starting, discuss in the seminar group what an outreach program is and what characteristics you want in a coordinator. Make a list of the characteristics for ready reference.

In your smaller groups read three letters of application for this position found in your resource package under Learning Guide 1.4. Consider the following as you read and then reach a group consensus as to whom you would hire for the position.

(1) What impression did you get of the applicant?

(2) Which applicant fits your requirements as found on the master list of characteristics?

(3) Where in the application do you see these characteristics demonstrated?

Once all groups have selected the successful applicant reconvene the seminar and present your selections and reasons.

Learning Activity #3

You enjoy personalizing your locker with posters and pictures. Your friends also like to have personalized lockers.

On Monday of this week the superintendent of schools walked through the halls of the school on an informal inspection. To him some student lockers were decorated with what he perceived as questionable material, i.e., drug/alcohol promotion, suggestive pictures, etc.

Your English teacher has told you that the principal will be making a P.A. announcement next week banning all pictures and posters in lockers.

You feel this is wrong. Write a letter to the principal expressing your concerns and try to get him to reconsider his decision.

Submit your letter to a teacher for evaluation. The letters will be sent to the principal who will be invited to the seminar on literary point of view to respond to them.

There are seven additional activities included in this learning guide. The approximate time budget for completing the entire guide is two to three weeks. Individual students may develop daily goal sheets as determined by a teacher designed to maintain progress through the guide. Goal sheets are usually three by five cards on which the students respond to three questions. (1) What do you intend to complete this "period"? (2) What did you complete this "period"? (3) Explain the reasons for any discrepancies. Students place the card in the upper right-hand corner of their work space so that a teacher can quickly and less obtrusively monitor individual progress.

VOCATIONAL / TECHNICAL EDUCATION

Vocational/technical education can be integrated into the regular curriculum. As students progress in the Specialized area of a subject area, they are expressing a desire to exceed the Essential and Desirable learnings. In Feldman's nomenclature they will pursue learning beyond the apprentice level. In many respects today's efforts to modernize vocational/technical education under the heading of Tech Prep is tacit recognition of the importance of individual interest and initiative in learning.

Tech Prep is shorthand for technical preparation. It provides technical preparation in engineering technology; applied science; mechanical, industrial or practical art or trade; agriculture; health or business. It marries academic and vocational skills designed to prepare students for college or additional technical/vocational training and a workplace/apprenticeship. By entering into an agreement with a community college, high school students can pursue college credit while still in high school or move easily to the next level of study in what has been labelled a 4 + 2 system or a 2 + 2 system, depending on when the student enters the sequence.

The Tech Prep programs usually include courses in applied algebra, geometry, economics, communication, chemistry, statistics and other subject areas deemed relevant to preparation for a life after high school. Students learn their academics in context and usually have little trouble connecting what they are asked to learn in school with the real world. At Hayes High School in Delaware, Ohio "teachers use a variety of teaching techniques (cooperative learning, team teaching, group projects, individual projects) and teaching tools (computers with CD-ROMs, video, color LCD panel, a camera that takes pictures on disk instead of film, Internet) that are commonly used by and available to many educators" (Rider, 1994, p. 20). Tech Prep uses hands-on learning through an integrated curriculum and requires each student to complete a major project each nine-week term (Rider, 1994). At St. Mary's, Pennsylvania, a School-to-Work package helped high school educators arrange a schedule so that Tech Prep students could be placed on the job two full days per week and back at school the other three days to work on their major subject areas (Clark, 1994). One of the premier Tech Prep programs in the nation, Richmond Senior High School in Richmond, North Carolina, describes two graduates of their 4 + 2 program. One of the graduates now serves as a field engineer for a computer company servicing more than 100 auto dealerships and the other earned a full scholarship to North Carolina State University.

The implementation of Tech Prep programs may vary slightly across states, school districts and schools; but there is one constant. The programs are built on the interests of individual students. Students are helped to see the relevance of what they are asked to study in school with their lives outside of school.

In an interview Edward Rensi, CEO of McDonald's USA, discussed the skills stressed by his company to provide employees with a jump-start to their careers. He cited time management, teamwork, cooperation, negotiation and self-discipline as attributes important for anyone. He recognized the importance of businesses working with educators to integrate classroom and work experience. In his mind the basic skills of reading, writing, speaking and listening need to be strengthened in all graduates regardless of career or vocational aspirations. The interesting phenomenon of the twenty-first century and beyond may well be that unlike our predecessors who saw the two paths of vocational and academic education diverging in the woods, the two areas are more alike than different. If so, our students may no longer have to choose one path at the expense of the other, but may combine a variety of experiences into a program of study suitable to their needs.

First Steps

Step One

Examine the various national reports which address standards in subject areas and standards across subject areas. Obtain a copy of the new edition of *The Systematic Identification and Articulation of Content Standards and Benchmarks* by John Kendall and Robert Marzano published by McREL in Aurora, Colorado. This document presents 157 standards and 1541 benchmarks arranged in four levels. Levels III and IV focus on grades 6–12. Standards are presented for science, mathematics, history, geography, communication, working with others, self-regulation and life work. This publication and the publications of national groups serve as excellent resources for establishing core competencies required for all students.

Step Two

Identify four to six broad competencies that seem essential for *all* students to participate effectively in the twenty-first century. Key stakeholders should have a voice in identifying the core competencies. These competencies should be required of all students as necessary for graduation with a standard diploma. For example, all students should develop facility in informational and recreational reading. Students will view reading as a lifelong learning skill. Mary Leonhardt's *Parents Who Love Reading, Kids Who Don't* (1993) is an excellent resource for helping create interest in reluctant readers.

Step Three

Obtain copies of subject area curriculum frameworks developed at the state level.

Step Four

Using the national standards and benchmarks and the state frameworks, form subject area teams to develop scopes and sequences for each school discipline and each course within the discipline. Depending on the nature of local situations, it is best to begin small, working with those teachers who are interested in reconceptualizing the curriculum. It is reasonable to begin with one subject area as a pilot which, once refined, can serve as a model for other subjects.

Step Five

When the pilot curriculum is in draft form, other teachers in the school and in the district should review it and give feedback as a form of quality control. Refine the material based on the feedback.

Step Six

Begin to develop units or learning guides for each of the major ideas or concepts contained in the curriculum. The units or guides should follow an acceptable format. The example of a learning guide in this chapter and the format for developing a learning guide in Chapter 5 offers one possibility. Allan Glatthorn (1994) suggests another described in "Constructivism: Implications for Curriculum."

CHAPTER 3

Instruction as a Means to Success for All Students

Give a man a fish and he can eat for a day
Teach a man to fish and he can eat for the rest of his life.—*Anonymous*

THE DEVELOPMENT OF curriculum standards serves to establish the content from which outcomes for each student are derived. Merely identifying those standards and the behaviors which, if mastered, will indicate a student has achieved the standards is only the initial step. In and of themselves, the standards do not assure that students will achieve them.

The notion of individual differences is hardly new. It is a phenomenon which has been discussed for decades but only a few high school programs are organized to take this notion seriously. Students are different in a number of important dimensions which relate to their ultimate success in school. Two important dimensions are their learning histories and their learning styles.

Learning history refers to their content background in various subject areas. It is contained in the information, skills, procedures and principles that are structured in long-term memory. It is also contained in the value which students attach to school generally and to specific subjects. These values are usually the result of the students' histories of relative success or failure in school.

Learning style refers to how students learn and how they like to learn. How they learn is the sum of their effectiveness in processing information for long-term retention and retrieval. Effective students direct and control the human information processing system successfully. They are well-grounded in the skills needed to control this system. Less successful students are either average or weak in the processing skills and hence are less likely to store information appropriately. Relative strength in these skills is crucial to the quality of meaning that each student gains from school experiences.

In an information society, information is the currency for active participation. Students who know how to process information effectively will be better prepared to take an active place in society. Students who do not will be destined to play a much lesser role. When students construct knowledge, they do so differentially, and within the constraints of individual talent, interests and abilities. It is the task of formal schooling to prepare each student to do so as well as possible. The skills with which students control the learning process affect the validity of how they construct knowledge and their ability to solve problems and generate new knowledge.

HUMAN INFORMATION PROCESSING

Letteri's general operations model of human information processing seems to describe what is needed to help students learn as well as anyone. According to Letteri (1988) learning is "a monitored, controlled and directed cognitive activity on the part of the individual, utilizing the information processing system of the brain for the purpose of modifying cognitive structures through assimilation and integration of new information" (p. 113). The key parts of this definition are: controlled and directed by the individual, and modification of cognitive structures or long-term memory. When students are able to take new information and assimilate it into what they already know or modify what they know to accommodate the new information, they are said to have learned. Anything less than this end result is temporary and often simply memorization, a process which retains information separate and apart from existing knowledge.

Human information processing begins when students respond to internal or external stimuli through one or more of the perceptual modalities. The manner in which information is presented may determine whether or not they respond to it. If they do not, then the event didn't happen. Assuming students respond in some form, then a decision is made to reject, memorize, transform or learn the material. Each decision results in a different set of behaviors. If the decision to reject the information is invoked then the information is dropped from the system. Students often reject information because it doesn't make sense, is uninteresting or is irrelevant. If students choose to memorize the material, then they initiate a procedure called maintenance rehearsal. This behavior is familiar to all of us. Information is repeated over and over again until it can be held in short-term memory for purposes of immediate recall, usually to pass a test. After the test is completed the information gradually leaves the system because it is not integrated into long-term memory.

If the decision is made to transform the material to something already known then it is held in working memory until it can be compared to existing information. Incorrect transformation of material results from (1) the failure to understand the material initially or (2) inaccurate filing of material in long-term memory. In either case, real learning has not occurred. If the student decides to learn the material, the information is compared and contrasted with existing information and integrated into existing cognitive structures.

The success of the entire human information process rests upon the ability of students to control and direct it. This ability is determined by their relative strength with the skills that control the system, namely, analyzing, spatial reasoning, focusing, categorizing, sequential processing, simultaneous processing and memorizing. All of these skills are integral to the system and influence the quality of learning. Weaknesses in one or several of these skills will diminish the student's ability to learn. When these weaknesses go undiagnosed for any length of time, students are unable to learn effectively and frequently develop negative attitudes toward schooling.

DIAGNOSING STUDENT LEARNING STYLES

Researchers have established the fact that students have different learning styles. They respond differently to the same learning environments. They present different demands on teachers who share responsibility for creating the learning environments. Diagnostic tools are now available to enable educators to diagnose the learning style profiles of high school students and to adjust instruction to the individual needs of students. In this context, needs are considered as adjustments that must be made to help students learn effectively. When instruction matches the unique learning characteristics of individual students, needs are more likely met. Adjusting instruction to students' learning styles facilitates the learning of new and difficult material.

There are many different models of learning style. The most comprehensive for use with high school students, however, has been developed by a task force of the National Association of Secondary School Principals (NASSP) in Reston, Virginia. The *Learning Style Profile* (LSP) is based upon a human information processing system. It acknowledges that the business of schooling is to help students acquire the knowledge and skills to succeed in the workplace. It also acknowledges that, to the degree that schools are able to provide learning environments sensitive to the learning style needs of students, more will do quality work.

The *LSP* assesses twenty-four elements of style representing four dimensions: cognitive skills, perceptual responses, study preferences and instructional preferences as follows.

Cognitive Skills

(1) Analysis—breaking information into its component parts so that it can be better understood
(2) Spatial—rotating objects in one's imagination; being able to attend to more aspects of an object because one sees it from different viewpoints
(3) Discrimination—focusing on relevant as opposed to irrelevant information; focusing on required details and avoiding distractions
(4) Categorization—forming accurate, complete and organized categories of information; using narrow rather than broad criteria in placing information in categories
(5) Sequential processing—the tendency to derive meaning from information presented in a step-by-step linear fashion
(6) Simultaneous processing—the tendency to grasp information all-at-once; seeing the big picture when only the parts are available
(7) Memory—detecting and remembering subtle changes in visual information; refers to short-term visual memory
(8) Verbal-spatial—preference for verbal or spatial tasks

The cognitive skills directly impact the student's ability to control and direct the information processing system. The results of students' performances on these eight scales provide insight into how well they can learn. Letteri (1988) estimates that much of the variation in student achievement can be attributed to strength or weakness in the cognitive skills.

Perceptual Response

(*1*) Visual—one's initial response to new information is visual

(*2*) Auditory—one's initial response to new information is auditory

(*3*) Emotive—one's initial response to new information is kinesthetic or emotional

These scales are based on the work of Harry Reinert (1976) in Edmonds, Washington. Reinert, a high school teacher of foreign languages, invented the *Edmonds Learning Style Identification Exercise* (ELSIE). His interest was in teaching students individually. By administering the *ELSIE* he gained information with which to adjust instruction to students. The perceptual response section of the *LSP* is an adaptation of the *ELSIE*. Most students have a dominant preference. How information is presented directly affects its reception by the human information process system. If information does not enter the system it can not be processed.

Instructional and Study Preferences

(*1*) Verbal risk—the willingness to express opinion and share points of view even in the face of opposition

(*2*) Persistence—willingness to work at a task until it is completed

(*3*) Manipulative—preference for "hands-on" activities

(*4*) Times of day—early morning, late morning, afternoon, and evening; four separate scales which indicate when a student has the most energy

(*5*) Grouping—preference for working in a class grouping of thirty, a small group of eight to fifteen, or in pairs or alone. It is sometimes referenced as a sociological preference

(*6*) Posture preference—preference for sitting on hard furniture (formal) or couches, pillows, the floor (informal) when working

(*7*) Mobility—preference for moving about or taking frequent breaks as opposed to sitting still for extended periods of time

(*8*) Sound—preference for quiet study areas versus areas with some background music when working

(*9*) Lighting—preference for bright versus dim lighting in study areas

(*10*) Temperature—preference for studying in a warm or cool environment

The instructional and study preferences offer students an opportunity to do their school work in circumstances that enhance their ability to attend to the learning task at hand. It is unlikely that students will identify all ten elements as necessary to keep them on task. Usually, students list three or four. In reviewing a student profile one looks for extremes not scores in the middle. Figure 3.1 shows a student profile based upon the results of the *LSP*.

THIS PROFILE IS FOR: AMY WALKER
BIRTHDATE: 11-22-82 SEX: F GRADE: 9 RACE: 2
DATE: 9-07-94 SCHOOL: 00010 CLASS:

SKILLS—GENERAL APPROACH TO PROCESSING INFORMATION

	SCORE	WEAK		AVERAGE		STRONG
ANALYTIC	60					XX
SPATIAL	40		XX			
DISCRIMINATION	56				XX	
CATEGORIZATION	71					XX
SEQUENTIAL	51				XX	
MEMORY	50			XX		
SIMULTANEOUS	48			XX		

PERCEPTUAL RESPONSES—INITIAL RESPONSE TO VERBAL INFORMATION

	SCORE	WEAK		AVERAGE		STRONG
VISUAL	61					XX
AUDITORY	39		XX			
EMOTIVE	55				XX	

ORIENTATIONS AND PREFERENCES—PREFERRED RESPONSE TO STUDY OR INSTRUCTIONAL ENVIRONMENT

	SCORE	LOW		AVERAGE		HIGH
PERSISTENCE	55				XX	
VERBAL RISK	28	XX				
MANIPULATIVE	44			XX		
STUDY TIME:						
EARLY MORNING	68					XX
LATE MORNING	56				XX	
AFTERNOON	46			XX		
EVENING	34	XX				

	SCORE		HIGH	NEUTRAL		HIGH	
VERBAL-SPATIAL	62	SPATIAL				XX	VERBAL
GROUPING	30	SMALL	XX				LARGE
POSTURE	57	INFORMAL			XX		FORMAL
MOBILITY	39	STILLNESS	XX				MOVEMENT
SOUND	45	QUIET		XX			SOUND
LIGHTING	58	DIM			XX		BRIGHT
TEMPERATURE	51	COOL		XX			WARM

CONSISTENCY SCORE: 3 NORMATIVE SAMPLE: NATIONAL

Figure 3.1. *Individual Student Learning Style Profile.*

The *LSP* is an untimed test with 126 items that can be administered in a group or individual setting. Typically, students take from thirty to sixty minutes to complete the test. It can be scored with a hand scoring answer sheet, a scoring disk or a main frame scoring package suitable for larger school districts.

The results of the profile for individual students can be used to plan for instruction. Ideally a plan would be developed for each student based upon the profile results. Alternative approaches to common objectives can be provided within the expertise and comfort level of the individual teacher. A team approach can allow for more flexibility and more input into the interpretation of the profiles.

ACCOMMODATING DIFFERENT LEARNING STYLE PROFILES

The first step in accommodating individual student learning style differences is to become well acquainted with the literature. Extensive reading can help develop an appropriate grounding in the concept. Having a school faculty or team take, score and interpret the *LSP* can also help. Some schools have formed inquiry teams in order to diagnose several students and then work collaboratively to create different teaching strategies for individual students.

Since the cognitive skills account for the major variation in school achievement addressing them first appears a logical initial step. A cognitive skills resource center can be established and staffed by a teacher especially trained to reduce deficiencies. Students with serious weaknesses in several of the skills could be scheduled for two to three hours per week for intensive augmentation. Letteri's research at the University of Vermont revealed that middle school students with weaknesses in several cognitive skills could be taught to improve the skills in thirty hours of training. After thirty hours of remediation the students improved their performances on a standardized test of mathematics by 3.75 grade levels (Letteri, 1982). An NASSP publication, *Developing Cognitive Skills* (Jenkins, Letteri, and Rosenlund, 1990) offers suggestions for enhancing each of the cognitive skills assessed by the *LSP*.

A second approach is to train classroom teachers to analyze their lesson plans to determine the cognitive skill requirements needed to understand the lesson and to succeed with any assignments. Once determined, the teachers can teach or reinforce the cognitive skill requirements to precede the lesson or integrated into the content of the lesson. Additionally, students with strengths in the specific skills can be paired with students who are weak in the skills to provide additional help. In a team setting one teacher could be designated the cognitive skills specialist.

Scores on the perceptual response elements help the teachers determine how to introduce new or difficult material to students. Introducing material through a student's strongest perceptual response mode and reinforcing it with the student's second strongest perceptual response mode seems the best technique. Visual learners prefer to receive information from pictures, transparencies, graphs, charts, videos and other visual media. They also respond favorably when conversation or presentations include words like look, see, imagine and other visual metaphors. Auditory learners respond best to what they hear. They like to listen to people talk about ideas, concepts and events. Lectures, audio tapes and discussions work well for them.

The emotive response mode is more complex than visual or auditory. Students who indicate a preference for the emotive response may be one of two types of learners. They may be learners who prefer information when it is presented kinesthetically. They often take notes or draw when viewing a video or listening to a presentation. These students need to be involved more directly in their learning. Field trips, hardware, machines, dramatizations and similar activities are appropriate. A second kind of emotive learner is one who has developed strong feelings toward school, specific subjects or people. They are students who pursue school very subjectively and are unable to separate emotion from content or context. Usually, the feeling is the result of an extended history of failure and it is negative. Before these students can learn successfully, they must be helped to overcome the negativism, and this takes time. Sometimes it requires a complete change in school environment.

The instructional and study preferences are the easiest to accommodate. Adding comfortable furniture to a classroom or seating students in bright or dimly lighted areas often present no problem. Cooperative group learning appears best suited for students who prefer to work in small groups. They are also effective for students with low verbal risk. Students who prefer to work alone can be assigned more independent study. Students with high mobility needs can be permitted to move about the room. Low persisters can have shorter assignments and more frequent breaks. Hands-on learning activities work best for students with preference for manipulatives. Time of day preferences can be accommodated in scheduling students to take difficult subjects when they have their highest energy level, if possible. Variations in temperature needs can be handled by encouraging students to wear warmer or cooler clothing.

Students can adjust to their study preferences when they are aware of their own styles and what they mean. Counseling students to understand their own styles is an important step in helping them to adjust when, where and how they study (see Griggs, 1991). Students with high energy in the early morning can be counseled to arrange study times accordingly. Students with informal design preferences can do their homework on comfortable furniture. Students with high mobility needs can be directed to take breaks from their study and to stand or walk about. A second NASSP publication *Accommodating Perceptual, Study and Instructional Preferences* offers additional suggestions on how to adjust the learning environment to individual student learning style preferences (Keefe, 1989).

MAKING CLASSROOMS SMARTER

Smarter classrooms and instructional areas are places where teachers diagnose student strengths and work to match the learning environment with individual student learning style characteristics. The diagnosis can be accomplished using a formal instrument such as the *LSP*, or can be done informally by observing students in a classroom. In either case, it is sensible to focus instruction on the strengths of students rather than their weaknesses except in cases of the cognitive skills deficiencies.

Given the individual differences among teachers, Table 3.1 provides a general description of the steps that can be taken to implement a program. These steps, however, are not rigid and more enterprising educators can begin at a more advanced stage.

More teachers can participate in a learning style program by starting with Step One and working toward Step Five. Adjusting for differences in instructional and study preferences does not require any change in how instruction is delivered. Teachers can continue to teach all students in the same way.

Table 3.1. Developmental Steps in Implementing a Learning Style Program.

Step One:	Teach all students similarly, but make adjustments in the classroom environment, e.g., optional furniture, dim/bright light areas, etc.
Step Two:	Teach all students similarly, but provide a variety of activities at the same time for all students.
Step Three:	Use small group learning strategies about 70 percent of the time as an alternative to traditional instruction.
Step Four:	Diagnose differences in learning style for one or more students. Adjust instruction accordingly.
Step Five:	Expand the diagnosis of style to all students. Establish writing teams to develop materials to accommodate styles in subject areas.

Step Two introduces instructional variety by design. Again the students are taught similarly. Overhead transparencies are used to supplement the spoken work when lecturing. Academic games involve students in discovering knowledge. Some hands-on activities can be developed for all students. The important consideration is variety of techniques. Students experience them simultaneously. There is no attempt to individualize. A commercial program which accomplishes this end is the 4-Mat System (McCarthy, 1981).

Step Three offers cooperative and competitive learning groups for all students. The smaller groups adjust to many learning style differences simultaneously, e.g., lighting, time of day, mobility, persistence and verbal risk. Students who prefer to work alone or in pairs can sometimes complete small group activities in this manner. Small group activities are easier for secondary teachers to implement and serve as a useful prelude to the diagnosis/prescriptive approach in Step Four.

Step Four is the start of personalized learning geared to the learning style needs of individual students. It is perhaps best to start with one or two students in order to practice administering an instrument, interpreting a profile and making adjustments in instruction. The decision to start small enables the teacher(s) to determine if the adjustments implemented result in the intended outcomes. Modifications can be made in light of the results.

Step Five is the implementation of a truly personalized learning approach (Keefe, 1984). Student learning styles are diagnosed and the results used to match instruction with individual student differences.

Students with cognitive skills weaknesses are identified and provided assistance. Classroom teachers teach cognitive skills prior to or along with content. Perceptual response preferences are used to introduce new and difficult material in different ways. Initially, some students hear a presentation or a tape; visual students read or see a videotape; kinesthetic students act out, take notes from an overhead or use a computer. All are exposed to the same information but in different ways. Learning circles, electroboards, task cards and other hands-on materials are used by students with a high need for manipulatives. Students work alone, in pairs, in learning teams or with a teacher. Objectives are held constant, but students achieve them differently.

LEARNING STYLE HELPS CONSTRUCT MEANING

Each student's quest to make sense of his experience ties clearly to his ability to process information effectively. The *LSP* offers high school educators an opportunity to diagnose salient student learning characteristics and to offer instruction based on the diagnosis. Consulting both NASSP handbooks on style (Keefe, 1989; Jenkins et al. 1990) appropriate accommodations can be developed. The *LSP* can help schools to help students access information more accurately and store it in long term-memory in such a way that it is available when needed.

With the advent of an information society, employment opportunities will be enhanced for those individuals who can deal with complexity. Solving problems and generating new knowledge will become the responsibility of an ever increasing number of people. School is the one place where learning how to learn is central. The growth of knowledge establishes a condition that makes traditional instruction obsolete. New knowledge in human variability enables schools to become centers for quality learning.

Adopting a learning style model and adapting it to local requirements is one approach to restructuring high schools. More important, however, is the realization on the part of high school educators of the importance for considering these differences to help more students achieve higher standards of performance. When the leaders of a school understand what learning style is about, they are able to apply that knowledge to the improvement of an individual school. They are not held hostage by others with special information, nor are their students who must continue to learn throughout their lifetimes.

First Steps

Step One

Arrange for a motivational presentation at a faculty meeting by someone who is well-grounded in learning style diagnosis and accommodation. Stress that the person making the presentation reference specific research that supports teaching to students' learning styles.

Step Two

Following the presentation invite interested faculty to a second session where they take, score, and profile the *Learning Style Profile* (LSP). Even though the results of the *LSP* are not valid for adults this step will give faculty an overview of the profile and will introduce ways to adjust to student learning style differences. Again, the person conducting this session should be one well-grounded in the use of the *LSP*.

Step Three

Bring the same interested group of teachers together and have them focus on interpreting case studies based on the *LSP*. In fact, from this point forward each staff development session should begin by placing student profiles on an overhead and discussing how to interpret them.

Step Four

Continue with the same group by examining ways to restructure classroom instruction to accommodate learning style differences. Using the two handbooks developed by NASSP offers directions for developing materials and procedures for teaching to style.

Step Five

Ask each teacher to identify one student that he or she is having the most trouble reaching. Using the hand scoring answer sheets, have the teachers administer the LSP to the identified students. If it is easier, the *LSP* could be administered by one person to all the identified students at one time. The teacher who identified the student, however, should score and profile the results.

Step Six

Arrange the teachers in inquiry groups and have them look at the individual profiles of the various students of the teachers in the particular group. Ask them to suggest ways to adjust instruction for each of the students. Armed with this information, the individual teachers should then develop a written plan for restructuring instruction for the student.

Step Seven

Have each teacher review his or her plans for the individual student with the members of his or her inquiry group. The plans should then be refined and ready for implementation.

Step Eight

Implement the plans for the students. The inquiry groups should continue to meet on a regular basis to share successes, problems and questions. Assuming each teacher will experience a degree of success with this approach, he/she can then extend the approach to other students. The point to keep in mind is that teachers need to have a successful experience from which to learn and from which to generalize.

Step Nine

As the project gains momentum other teachers should be invited to participate. The initial group of teachers can plan the staff development to orient the new teachers to the learning style program. From the outset it is necessary that the principal and other school leaders visibly participate in the program. It is the wise principal who actually shares responsibility for teaching the faculty or at the least participates as a learner him/herself.

Step Ten

Develop a professional library of books, monographs, articles and materials about learning style. The following might serve as a starting point:

- Keefe, J. W. *Learning Style Theory and Practice*, NASSP, 1987.
- Keefe, J. W., ed. *Profiling and Utilizing Learning Style*, NASSP, 1988.
- Jenkins, J. M., C. A. Letteri, and P. Rosenlund. *Developing Cognitive Skills*. NASSP, 1990.
- Keefe, J. W. *Accommodating Perceptual and Instructional Preferences*, NASSP, 1989.
- Staff development materials from the Learning Styles Network, St. John's University, Jamaica, New York.

CHAPTER 4

Creative Thinking Students: Today's Social Imperative

> The most striking feature of our schools is that the quality of the students they graduate is mostly a function of the background of the students they enroll. . . . A truly good school would be one that graduated students who are more successful than would be predicted by their social class.—*Ray Marshall and Marc Tucker (1992)*

WHEN ONE ANALYZES the impact of technology on the demands of the workplace, it becomes increasingly clear that the traditional systems of education will not work. As technological advances create new jobs and make others obsolete, the dialectic of destruction and creation is producing a world in which the unskilled worker will become an anachronism.

Traditional high school programs were designed for a different time and a different economy. Mass production, personified by the assembly line, assumed that the persons who assembled the products would follow the lead of those who supervised the process. Thinking was the domain of management, not the worker.

The educational system created to support the model of mass production educated the "brightest and the best" to assume responsibilities for leadership. Similar to the current approach to gifted education, abler students were separated early in the educational process and provided an appropriately challenging education. Students were tracked or ability-grouped with the curricula designed to "meet their academic needs." Higher-order thinking activities were reserved for those students who seemed predestined for leadership. In this system the rich literally got richer. Students who came to the high school with enriched backgrounds were more likely to find their way into the upper tracks or the higher ability classes.

Educating a minority of students for leadership seems out of touch with the needs of today's global economy. Rapid economic growth worldwide has placed our standard of living in peril. We cannot survive economically in a global market without standards of education which give high priority to educating all students to think critically. Jobs which were once appropriate for the less educated are being done by machines. The military no longer provides a refuge for dropouts. It takes a thoughtful recruit to deal with sophisticated systems of weaponry and navigation. Even the service industry requires that employees think on their feet and adjust to a variety of unpredictable circumstances.

TEACHING FOR THINKING

Teaching all students to be effective thinkers seems best accomplished if one thinks of thinking in terms of a continuum of skills ranging from basic to higher order. Keefe (1992) provides such a framework as shown in Figure 4.1.

The *cognitive skills* (analysis, discrimination, categorization, spatial reasoning, sequential processing, simultaneous processing and memory) are the building blocks of thinking. They form the foundation for the acquisition, storage and retrieval of information. Weaknesses in one or several of these skills can have serious negative ramifications at the other levels. Fortunately all of these skills are improvable through training.

The *learning-to-learn* level involves using the cognitive skills effectively in order to learn. As students develop their cognitive skills, they must learn to manage these skills in the service of learning. Students must be taught how to transfer the cognitive skills to a variety of different situations; it does not happen automatically.

Cognitive Skills	Learning-to-Learn	Content Thinking	Reflective Reasoning
Basic			Higher-order

Figure 4.1. Levels of Information Processing Skills.

Content thinking combines the use of cognitive skills and the use of their management to process subject matter content effectively. "Such skills as concept attainment . . ., pattern recognition and synthesizing enable learners to understand and learn new concepts to comprehend, organize and integrate new bodies of knowledge" (Keefe, 1992, p. 123).

Reflective is the highest form of thinking. It incorporates all of the preceding levels so that the learner can make judgments to restructure previous understandings and to generate new knowledge. In essence, it gives the individual a higher elevation from which to operate—a different perspective on reality. It need not be the exclusive property of the students enrolled in advanced programs.

It is likely that students have different skills at many places on the continuum. A student can have strong analytic skills and weak discrimination skills, average learning-to-learn skills, very weak content application skills and good critical thinking skills made possible by the strength in analysis. In this case, however, "the higher-order capability is limited to a form that relates to everyday thinking, a type of thinking which often requires higher-order thinking capabilities" (Keefe, 1992, p. 120).

Weaknesses at the lower levels can cause weaknesses at other points on the continuum. Students with weaknesses in simultaneous processing will be less able to detect relationships. Students with weak learning-to-learn skills will struggle as they attempt to understand subject matter. Even poor performance in certain subject areas can be directly linked to weaknesses in specific cognitive skills.

One piece of the thinking puzzle that appears to be missing from Keefe's continuum centers on readying the mind for serious study. New findings in the cognitive sciences have suggested a close relationship between mind and body. In fact the closeness of this relationship might best be described by creating a new word, mind-body.

The mind-body is by its nature random, not orderly—a condition once described by the psychologist William James as a "booming, buzzing, confusion" from which individuals must develop adequate behaviors to gain control. According to University of Chicago psychologist Mihalyi Czikszentmihalyi (1990), this natural state of chaos leads the mind to follow random patterns, usually stopping to consider something painful or disturbing.

For many high school students calming the mind must precede activities to understand subject matter. Very often students who do poorly in school are students who do not seem able to attend to the tasks at hand. Given the concept of mind-body, their hyperactivity may be an outer manifestation of an underlying uneasiness which must be addressed prior to engaging the continuum of thinking behavior. Including activities which both calm and order the mind-body may be a necessary first step. Introducing students to the rote memorization of poetry, verse or prose can order their consciousness by imposing the order of an author's mind. Such thinking dates back to Plato who believed that students should be taught music first because the harmonies and rhythms would order their consciousness.

IMPLEMENTING A THINKING PROGRAM

As Sir Winston Churchill observed, "we shape our institutions and then they shape us." Helping all students to improve higher-order thinking is a total school function. It is not the domain of one program or a cluster of advanced courses. Keefe's continuum of thinking offers specifications for determining necessary activities to advance the cause of higher-order thinking for all. The continuum provides an advanced organizer for program planning and pedagogical decisions.

Administering the *Learning Style Profile* can provide initial information on each student's relative strength in each of the cognitive skills. Students with weaknesses in one or more of the skills can be scheduled for a part of their week into special programs to alleviate these weaknesses. Identifying a member of the faculty as a cognitive resource teacher to function similarly as a reading resource teacher is a first step. This person provides direct help to all students identified as needing cognitive skills strengthening. Needy students can be scheduled with the cognitive resource teacher for one to two hours each week, either individually or in groups. While augmenting students' cognitive skills, the cognitive resource teacher also helps them to use the skills in combination and teaches them how to transfer the skills to subject matter content.

When other teachers are aware of students' cognitive skills needs, they can reinforce the skills in subject matter teaching and assist with the transfer. All teachers who have contact with students must recognize their cognitive skills proficiencies and deficiencies. In that way they can offer instruction that accommodates the learning needs of individual students. Moreover, teachers in content areas can be challenged to integrate the thinking activities into content teaching. For example, instructional activities can be analyzed to determine the cognitive requirements for succeeding with the learning task. Comparing the cognitive requirements with individual student profiles enables the teachers to determine logical next steps for helping individual students succeed with the learning task.

In addition, the cognitive resource teacher can work with teachers to create activities which focus on content thinking and reflective reasoning. Building bridges to reflective reasoning can be enhanced when courses are organized around questions or exhibitions that require students to apply content in predictive and nonpredictive circumstances. Teachers can show students the processes they use when thinking reflectively and then ask students to do the same. Teachers can also insist that students use precise language in describing their thinking processes. Words like predict, hypothesize and conclude should be used in this discourse. Teachers can demonstrate the use of mnemonics when memorization of material is required. Students can be expected to adopt the thinking behaviors of historians, mathematicians, chemists and biologists in ways reminiscent of the inquiry-based programs of the 1960s. Each discipline has its own heuristics for interpreting experiences and generating new knowledge. In this context students can be expected to assume the roles of the major performers.

Curriculum is the work plan by which the teachers implement a thinking program. Specific outcomes for thinking should be identified in order to focus and connect the work of the teachers. These outcomes can be single or multidisciplinary in scope. Either way, when outcomes for thinking are clearly stated and included in the curriculum expectations, it is more likely that the teachers will integrate thinking skills and strategies into their teaching.

Testing should be expanded to include more authentic measures than the typical objective tests developed by teachers. These tests, aside from possessing questionable validity and reliability, are often exercises that measure the selection of right answers rather than an understanding of the content. The understanding of content seems better measured by assessment activities which require students to apply knowledge, defend their answers, create strategies to solve problems and combine information into new forms. It may also be measured by carefully constructed portfolios of quality student work. Discussions between students and teachers in which standards for quality work are articulated seem fitting preludes to such portfolio building. They are not just folders in which student work samples are placed. Students should have the opportunity of returning to any piece of work to improve its quality. No grade should be considered final.

CREATING A THINKING CULTURE

Every high school reflects the collective values of its constituents. It is a venue for learning. What is to be learned in this venue is determined by a corpus of influences both internal and external. Given the mood of the larger culture, however, an opportunity currently exists which facilitates the establishment of a thinking culture in the high school. The following excerpt from Goal Three of *America 2000* reads, "every school in America will ensure that all students learn to use their minds well. . . ." The inclusion of the verb *ensure* should be noted. There appeared to be a sense of urgency in this message from the President and the fifty governors that demanded an assurance that this important work would get done.

Like any organization, a high school is comprised of a myriad of elements all influencing what may be labelled as the school culture or climate. What may appear on the surface to be a separate entity, however, can be viewed at another level as a collection of energy fields all contributing to the totality. Whether one sees the school culture as a single entity or as a composite of energies, the impact on the behavior of its participants is deep. The culture is, in part, created by extending a vision statement for thinking to all corners of the high school. The more areas involved, the more intense the impact on individual behavior. Metaphorically, the message of thinking should be broadcast to the total school just as morning announcements on the public address or the closed-circuit television systems. No one should escape its influence.

The value of thinking should reside in all the school's activities. A discipline system which teaches students control theory and requires them to write behavioral contracts to correct irresponsible actions stresses thinking (see Chapter 8). Socratic seminars focus students' attention on important documents and other thoughtful works of literature. Classroom meetings require students to interact on provocative topics as well as ways to improve the process of their education (see Chapter 9). Additional student interactions are structured through cooperative and competitive group strategies in instructional settings.

Group problem solving gives students the opportunity to see that there is more than one way to achieve a desirable goal. Cooperative science projects extend the science fair concept to a larger participative audience of students. Writing across the curriculum stresses the importance of good writing regardless of the subject matter. Formulating school rules through open discussions helps students see the value of participatory decision making. Community-based learning experiences for all students link subject matter with real-life pursuits. Teachers engaging in action research projects to improve their teaching practices model reflective reasoning.

In some cases thinking may be taught in a specialized format. Commercially developed programs, such as *CoRT* (Cognitive Research Trust) help students to develop lateral or creative thinking strategies. *Project Impact* aims to teach problem solving and critical thinking. *Tactics for Thinking* includes learning-to-learn, content thinking and reasoning strategies that seem to parallel Keefe's thinking continuum. *Cognetics* provides learning activities which develop higher-order thinking skills through creative projects. All of these programs are worthwhile and will add to a high school's overall thinking efforts for all students. They should supplement and not supplant the school's thinking program.

While Keefe's thinking continuum may appear to be a linear concept, students function at all levels concurrently. Their relative strengths and weaknesses at one level affects their achievement at another. A student with weaknesses in several of the cognitive skills can still experience course work which demands higher level thinking. The depth of this thinking, however, may be limited accordingly. Students may enroll in one of the specialized thinking programs, but their progress will be determined by their facility at the basic thinking skills level.

STUDENTS AS KNOWLEDGE GENERATORS

Thinking students are not simply consumers of knowledge. The demands of the information age require that they also be creators of new knowledge. This new role is not the exclusive province of a cognitive elite, but rather a necessity for all citizens both as a requirement of citizenship and a requirement for employment. Students are bombarded by an increasing number of symbols on a daily basis. Making sense of these symbols seems the newest developmental task of youth.

In the 1940s Robert Havighurst coined the term "developmental tasks of life" to describe those things that constitute healthy and satisfactory growth in our society. He saw these tasks as contextual in that they arose at a specific period in a person's life and were bound by the nature of the societal demands. They arose from "physical maturation, from the pressures of culture processed upon the individual, from the desires, aspirations and values of the emerging personality" (Havighurst, 1948, p. 6). Physical tasks were related to learning to walk or learning to behave acceptably toward the opposite sex in adolescence. Cultural tasks could be found in learning to read and learning to be a responsible citizen. Choosing a vocation or a profession was an example of a task rooted in personal values and aspirations.

In addition to making sense of the complexity of twenty-first century living, today's youth must also become generators of new information. In the truest sense, all humans generate new information continuously as they construct meaning from experience. Establishing the personal conditions for creating new knowledge means more, however, than simply the idiosyncratic nature of existence. It means combining information in unique and creative ways. It means seeing the world from various perspectives. It means pushing the limits of artificial barriers which appear to separate knowledge. It means constructing new realities. In the past, these tasks have been linked with the creative process.

Activities to develop the creative process are often reserved for those students traditionally identified as gifted or for students enrolled in high-ability classes. The sheer volume of information available today seems to necessitate offering these activities to a wider audience. All students must cultivate the creative process. They must learn how knowledge is structured so that they can produce information as well as understand what it means.

What does this imperative mean for instruction? Initially, all teachers can be helped to help students see that all content has structure. Textbooks and other resource materials can be analyzed to determine the format that they use in presenting that structure. What information is essential and what is irrelevant detail are key questions teachers can use. Additionally, students can compare their own explanations of events and phenomena with the principles and laws specific to a given discipline.

Presenting concepts structurally enables students to see them from a broader perspective and to relate them to other concepts more readily.

Concept Structure			
Denotative	Connotative	Example	Episodic
Describes the concept in terms of its characteristics, operations, use	Assigns some feeling emotion or value to the concept	Offers an example, a synonym or an alternative for the concept	Describes a personal or vicarious experience with the concept

Figure 4.2. Format for Representing the Structure of a Concept.

For example, Figure 4.2 represents a structure that can be used to help students understand concepts beyond the typical school practice of writing and memorizing facts and definitions.

By describing the structure of a concept in this manner, students can broaden their understanding enabling them to discover more relationships. When they develop the habit of describing all important concepts in this manner, relationships between and among concepts can be more easily discovered. It is out of these relationships that new knowledge is generated. Knowledge present in one concept combines with knowledge present in another to create something totally new for the learner and at times totally new for a particular discipline.

The creative individual has been distinguished as a person who: (1) is not rigidly attached to one point of view; (2) judges from a personal frame of reference; (3) functions well in the midst of chaos and confusion; (4) sees the universe, including himself or herself, as intelligent; and (5) detects relationships that others miss. Previous wisdom attributed these traits to genetics. New discoveries in the cognitive sciences oblige a more optimistic conclusion. Every student is capable of developing habits of mind that provoke deeper meaning from divergent sources of information.

THE MESSAGE OF CONSTRUCTIVISM

Persons attempt to make sense of their personal circumstances. They operate from an internal frame of reference which is the product of the cumulative experiences that they have had in the process of growing up. It is through this frame of reference that people interpret new experiences. Thus, when students are confronted with learning tasks, they do so with preconceived ways of operating, interpreting and understanding. Principal in each student's education should be the opportunity to express those preconceptions safely and to compare them with the perceptions of others.

The construction of knowledge seems to occur best when students are faced with meaningful problems. Problems also enable students to determine what information they need to know and what information is relevant for solving the problems. For example, students at one high school wrote a history of their community. In a team effort twenty-three students devoted six months to interviewing people, conducting library research and writing a rough draft for their editor-teachers. The ninety-seven page finished product was then published and shelved for posterity at the public library and local historical society (Stacy, 1994).

Problem-focused learning permits students to use knowledge in pursuit of solutions. Students have the advantage of working side-by-side with other students, even teachers, for the purpose of creating new knowledge. This type of in-depth learning increases students' previous understanding of content and builds pathways to the future. The future will belong to those students who know how to learn and know how to think critically, know how to identify and solve problems and know how to invent new knowledge. A thinking continuum which begins with the basics and advances to behaviors of reflective reasoning is not only possible for all students, it is imperative.

First Steps

Step One

The cognitive skills domain of the *Learning Style Profile* (*LSP*) provides initial information about students' relative strengths and weaknesses in eight cognitive skills. Students who show weakness in one or more of these skills are at a disadvantage when learning tasks rely on strengths in these areas. Initial diagnosis of students with weaknesses leads to additional diagnoses to confirm the weaknesses. These additional diagnoses may take the form of more intensive testing using tests designed to assess specific skills, such as the *Embedded Figures Test* (analysis) or the *Cognitive Control Battery, Leveling-Sharpening House Test* (memory), the careful inspection of student work and/or the observations of teachers.

Step Two

Identify a teacher to serve as a cognitive skills resource teacher to the total school. Usually teachers with background in exceptional student education can be further trained to provide assistance to individual and small groups of students with cognitive skills weaknesses. They can also serve as consultants to teachers as they attempt to determine the cognitive skill requirements of specific learning tasks. The NASSP handbook, *Developing Cognitive Skills,* provides useful background for an incipient program.

Step Three

Work with a small group of interested teachers to analyze classroom learning tasks for the cognitive skill requirements. Very often students who do poorly on assignments do so because they lack the necessary skills. Combining this activity with the results of the *LSP* enables teachers to predict what students need preliminary augmentation prior to attempting the learning task.

Step Four

Pairing students with weak skills with students with strong skills can help students to complete learning tasks successfully and ostensibly improve their skills in the process.

Step Five

Students who require calming in order to ready their minds for thinking are often helped by reading well-written short stories, essays or memorizing poems. The repetition of the poetry tends to calm the mind. The reading of well-written prose can impose a mental order that students have difficulty imposing themselves.

Step Six

Establish inquiry groups of four to five teachers to develop ways to encourage thinking in subject areas. They could investigate various commercial materials to determine their usefulness or they might adapt some activities from these materials to their own curricula.

PART THREE

ORGANIZING THE HIGH SCHOOL

CHAPTER 5

New Realities and Old Paradigms

Some men see things as they are and say, why. I dream things that never were and say, why not.—*George Bernard Shaw*

IN THE DEDICATION to the revision of their book *The Nongraded Elementary School* (1963) Goodlad and Anderson wrote, "To our children in the hope that their children will come to know graded schools only through their history books." The idea of the nongraded school is based on the belief that children of similar chronological age are not ready for the same academic challenges at the same time. They come to school from an array of backgrounds and experiences. It was reasoned that a new form of school organization was necessary to take these differences into consideration to enable each student to experience success in the school setting.

In many respects the rationale for nongrading a school could have been written to support a constructivist paradigm for schooling. It is perhaps instructive that the work of Piaget was often referenced in the literature supporting the nongraded school. He described learners as going through the same stages of development in a fixed order. In infancy the child comes to know the world in a sensorimotor way. Next, the child goes through a preoperational stage and at seven or eight the concrete operational stage emerges. When the child reaches adolescence, he or she puts away "childish things" and advances to the formal operational stage where concepts are engaged more abstractly. Each stage of Piaget's model of human development represents a qualitatively different way of thinking and of constructing knowledge. He conceptualized only one broad aim for education – the development of autonomy (Kamii, Clark, and Dominick, 1994).

The nongraded educators believed that while Piaget's stages might describe a uniform sequence of cognitive development students did not necessarily go through them in the same time frame. In any chronological age grouping one might find children at different stages of development. In a graded classroom, it was not unusual to find extreme differences among students in a variety of academic tasks. Schools, therefore, needed to be reorganized if these important differences were to be acknowledged and if all students were to become successful learners. Failure could be eliminated if the school organization could adjust to differences among and within students.

Early efforts at nongrading the high school organized curricula in phases to correspond to what students knew at a given time in their lives. The number of phases depended on the size of the school and the nature of the subject matter. For example, phase one in a subject area was for students who were experiencing extreme difficulty. Phase two was one step up from the basics and the upper phases were for students who were at "grade level" or beyond. The placement of students was appropriate to the skills and background they brought to a particular discipline. As they advanced in their learning, they moved to the next phase. Changing students from one grouping to another was fluid.

The use of the term *phase* was deliberate, denoting a "temporary stage of development" that led naturally to the next higher one (Buffie and Jenkins, 1971). Offering students what they needed to succeed in a subject was viewed as a jump-start for further learning. Movement among phases was upward and not a means for students with a stronger knowledge base to gain easy credit. This principle presumed that the teachers and other school leaders were familiar with individual students well enough to intervene appropriately when unwise requests for schedule changes or course selections were made. Curriculum was developed along continua which assumed that what was learned at one juncture prepared the student for subsequent learning (Buffie and Jenkins, 1971).

Nongrading was more than a matter of organizational restructuring. It required redefining the curriculum so that simpler knowledge was antecedent to more complex knowledge. Higher-order thinking was a matter of integrating new learning into extant cognitive structures. What was considered basic and what was considered complex was an individual student matter. One way to reconceptualize subject matter can be seen in Figure 5.1, an example of a standard and its accompanying benchmarks in mathematics.

Standard: Understands and applies basic and advanced properties of functions in algebra.

Benchmarks

Phase I   Identifies basic number patterns

Phase II   Has a basic understanding of the concept of the variable
Interpolates simple patterns of numbers
Extrapolates simple patterns of numbers

Phase III   Understands the basic features of mathematics expressions
Understands the basic features of coordinates
Has a basic understanding of the concept of equation
Understands the characteristics and uses of the concept of rectangular coordinates
Solves problems involving rectangular coordinates
Solves problems involving formulas with one variable

Phase IV   Has a basic understanding of the concept of function
Understands the characteristics and uses of basic trigonometric functions
Has a basic understanding of the concept of inequalities
Has a basic understanding of parameters and their effects on curve shape
Understands that a correlation measures the linear relationship between two sets of data
Has a basic understanding of polynomial equations
Understands basic trigonometry functions
Solves problems involving polar coordinates
Determines the maximum points on a graph
Fits a line to a set of points
Fits a curve to a set of points

Figure 5.1. A Nongraded Approach to a Mathematics Standard and Its Supporting Benchmarks. Adapted from Kendall and Marzano (1994), The Systematic Identification and Articulation of Content Standards and Benchmarks.

Students are placed in one of the four phases for achieving this standard based upon their achievement of the specific benchmarks. Their progression through the standard is determined by demonstrated accomplishments. Standards are associated with specific courses in the high school curriculum or simply as standards which students mastered prior to graduation. Instruction is varied and appropriate to the diagnosed learning needs of each student.

During the 1960s it appeared that the nongraded or multiaged classroom school would become the norm for K–12 schools. It simply made so much sense. Parents with more than one child at home were quick to recognize the wisdom resident in the concept of individual differences. Schools which adopted the nongraded approach received much publicity and were visited by literally thousands of educators. Why the idea didn't take hold is a mystery. Perhaps it was a casualty of the "back to basics" movement or maybe it suffered from the absence of a common paradigm. One writer, Miller (1967), observed, "there are probably as many different kinds of nongraded schools as there are school systems experimenting with the notion." Given today's ethos the nongraded high school may be an idea whose time has arrived.

Contemplated changes in a high school's organizational structure are predicated on the contribution the changes will make to increased student productivity in the short run and potential for life success in the long view. Improved outcomes for students should be the primary focus of school reorganization. The old high school paradigm based on group teaching, the normal distribution curve mentality, rewards and punishments and uniform time frames seems out of step with the new discoveries in cognitive science and the projected contingencies for the future.

THE SHAPE OF A NONGRADED HIGH SCHOOL

When one examines the basic premises supporting the nongraded high school movement of the past, similarities with the premises supporting the constructivist approach to high school restructuring are evident. Before articulating these similarities, however, one disclaimer appears necessary. Nongradedness does not mean that the evaluation of student work is eschewed. On the contrary, judging the quality of student work is important. Nongradedness takes issue with the practice of grouping students arbitrarily on the criterion of chronological age. This practice results in labels such as ninth, tenth, eleventh and twelfth grade in considering student placement and courses in the curriculum.

In the nongraded high school, placement of students for instruction is based on criteria such as interest, demonstrated competencies, learning style and achievement rather than chronological age or years in school. For example, in concert band a student's age is insignificant to his or her ability to play an instrument. Who is assigned first chair in a section of the band is based on demonstrated competency. Resource centers to help students with skill deficiencies are available in reading, writing, mathematics and cognitive processing skills. Entry into ecological studies is often a matter of interest. Choices of learning tasks may be based on student achievement in a given subject area.

Students progress at their own rate within reasonable limits. The Carnegie unit is redefined or replaced by more meaningful indicators of student accomplishment. Credit is not based on seat time. Learning is viewed as continuous and positive. Students receive credit for what they know and what they have done. In traditional terms if they have completed sixty percent of a course, they get credit for sixty percent and move forward. They do not receive a failing grade and repeat the course totally.

Annual promotion and retention practices are eliminated. Failure is controlled by blending student placement with appropriate curriculum and instruction. Diagnosis of student strengths and weaknesses help the faculty determine the most appropriate placement for individual students. Teachers, therefore, relate more closely to students in order to facilitate diagnosis and prescriptive teaching.

Learning is an individual enterprise. Personal attention to each learner's needs takes the place of the practice of group teaching in many cases. Instruction takes place in groups of varying sizes, which, in some cases, change from day to day or week to week. Independent study is an option for many students. Students are not classified as slow learners or gifted or college-bound. Labels are avoided because they limit potential and often lead to self-fulfilling prophecies. Teachers have time to meet with students one-on-one.

There is a conscious effort to recognize and to give consideration to human variability. One lesson, one course, one method and one set of requirements do not fit all students. Textbooks are only one of a multiplicity of sources of information. Assessment is broadened beyond paper and pencil tests to demonstrations, presentations, problems to solve, experiments, research projects, dramatizations and sundry other indicators of student learning. The primary goal of the nongraded high school is to help all students become increasingly more independent of outside stimulation for learning.

All students are well-known by at least one professional on the school staff. Information about a student's interests, academic background and learning needs is disseminated to teachers on a need-to-know basis.

FOCUSING ON THE INDIVIDUAL STUDENT

Several organizational strategies enable teachers to focus instruction on individual students. One such strategy has its roots in the famous *Dalton Laboratory Plan of 1921*. The *Dalton Laboratory Plan* supplanted traditional classrooms with laboratories designated for specific academic disciplines. Students worked in the laboratories completing monthly contracts. They met each morning with their homeroom teachers who helped them select the contracts on which they wanted to work and scheduled their time in the appropriate laboratories (Edwards, 1991). This arrangement later became known as a teacher adviser plan.

In 1924 the first formal teacher adviser program was begun at New Trier High School in Winnetka, Illinois. The *Adviser-Personnel Plan* was "designed to provide educational, vocational, social, moral and ethical guidance and counsel to all the students of the school" (Clerk, 1928). The teacher adviser at New Trier was integral to helping each student reach his or her potential.

The need for working more closely with individual high school students has not abated over the years. In fact with the increasing diversity of high school student populations and with the size of many high schools the need has increased. High schools can be improved by simply focusing on individual students. Typically, among a high school support staff are one or more counselors trained to deliver guidance services to the total student body. One counselor may be assigned from 250 to 600 different students to counsel and advise which frequently precludes any meaningful interaction. Each student benefits from individual contact and attention on school concerns, but under the traditional arrangement, it is unlikely that anything other than a cursory meeting between a counselor and a student can occur.

In traditional organizations high school students see the guidance counselor only in group meetings, rarely one-to-one. Consequently, for a growing number of students, important questions go unanswered or are asked of less knowledgeable staff members. By reorganizing guidance services into a team effort with teachers and administrators serving as advisers to fifteen to twenty advisees, each student receives individual attention throughout his or her high school career. Figure 5.2 offers a general model for achieving this end.

This model places 300 students, one counselor and fifteen teacher advisers in each school cluster for delivering guidance services. The number of cluster groupings in each school will depend on the number of students enrolled. The counselors serve as "advisers to the advisers" and model their behavior accordingly. They meet with advisers on a one-to-one basis; they conduct appropriate staff development activities; they monitor the progress of individual students through each ad-

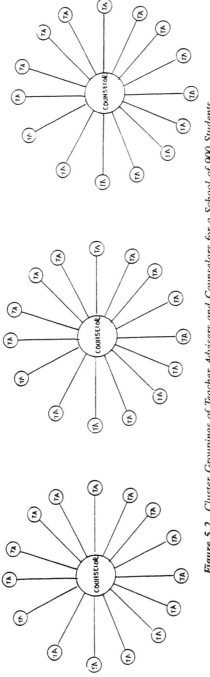

Figure 5.2. Cluster Groupings of Teacher Advisers and Counselors for a School of 900 Students.

viser. The communication between the counselors and their cluster advisers is a critical ingredient to the success of the program. The role of the teacher adviser is described in Chapter 6.

Advisees generally remain with their counselors and their teacher advisers for the duration of their high school years. Assignment of students to advisers can be done randomly or by request. Allowing students to choose the adviser with whom they plan to spend three or four years seems the better of the two choices although it has a downside. When students choose their advisers, popular teachers tend to get oversubscribed and some teachers rarely get chosen. Additionally, new students to the school have no basis for selecting an adviser.

In essence, the advisory group, teacher adviser and fifteen to twenty advisees can be viewed as a school-within-a-school. The adviser is the principal; the advisees are the students. The close working relationship of adviser and advisees enables each student to take full advantage of the school's resources and offers a ratio small enough for each student to be known as a "total human being" educationally.

A second strategy for focusing on individual students offers several variations on the theme that "small is better." Small schools enable more students to win because there are as many leadership roles in a small school as there are in a large school. High schools, regardless of size, have student body presidents, club presidents, team captains and band officers. The value of the smaller school is that the principal and other educators tend to know the students better and as a result can intervene at the slightest provocation or guide a student into more or less challenging academic settings as appropriate.

The trend toward large consolidated high schools or large urban high schools tends to exacerbate the problem of anonymity that befalls many students in today's high schools. Given the economic reasons for building larger high schools, the school-within-a-school offers a possible alternative. By reassigning assistant principals to serve as the principals of smaller schools within a larger high school, the positive characteristics of smallness can be recaptured. Faculty can be assigned to each of the schools and can be shared where special areas of teaching exist. The faculty and staff of the school-within-a-school work together as a team planning educational opportunities for each of the students in the smaller school. The fact that the students are still students of the larger high school enables facilities and resources to be shared while retaining the value of the small, more personable school. The total school principal then works with each smaller school principal to coordinate activities of the larger school.

A school of 1600 students can be divided into four schools of 400 or two schools of 800 or whatever variation the overall staffing of the school allows. Where there are not sufficient administrators to assign one to each smaller school, lead teachers can be chosen. In some cases the appointment of lead teachers for each of the smaller schools might prove a better arrangement. The school administration would then be free to provide services to all of the schools.

The school-within-a-school team arrangement brings teachers from different disciplines together (Table 5.1). Most high schools are currently organized in departments by subject areas. The English teachers meet with other members of the English department. Mathematics teachers meet together and on through the different subject areas. With the trend toward outcomes, exhibitions and performance-based learning the departmental arrangement may be waning. Outcomes focus on

Table 5.1. School-within-a-School (each school contains ninth, tenth, eleventh and twelfth grade students—using traditional nomenclatures).

	Alpha	Beta	Gamma	Sigma
Number of students	400	400	400	400

A School-within-a-School Team	Staff Teachers for Total School	Other Personnel
Lead teacher	2 Music teachers	1 Principal
4 English	2 Art teachers	2,3 Assistant
4 Social studies	2 Media specialists	principals
4 Mathematics	3,4 Foreign language	Paraprofessionals
4 Science	teachers	Secretaries
1 Counselor	4 Physical education	Custodial staff
	teachers	
	1 Reading resource	
	teacher	
	1 Cognitive skills resource	
	teacher	
	4,5 Vocational or prevoca-	
	tional specialists	

what students are able to do as a result of learning; and, what they do may not be restricted to one academic discipline. The Coalition of Essential Schools recommends four departments intead of the traditional eight or nine (see Sizer, 1992, Chapter Ten). At the least, consideration should be given to breaking down the isolation so prevalent in high schools.

THE ROLE OF THE PRINCIPAL

Historically the term *principal* was an Americanization of the British headmaster. We called our version the principal teacher. He or she was originally elected by the faculty to take care of the business of getting the school door opened and the chalk out and ready for the day. The selection was usually made because the teacher was considered the best teacher in the school, ergo, the term principal teacher. Jesse Stuart in *The Thread That Runs So True*, his classic account of education in rural Kentucky in the 1930s, describes his role as the principal teacher of a rural Kentucky high school in the 1930s. In addition to his duties as principal, he taught a full load of classes. Later he became principal of another high school and the term principal teacher was changed to simply principal. The adjective to describe the best teacher in the school was diminished to a noun removing the person from direct teaching responsibilities.

Beginning in the 1970s and accelerating through the 1980s the message of the principalship was one of instructional leader. This metaphor described principals who were actively involved in challenging the faculty and the community to improving instruction for each student. The principals were seen as *agent provocateurs* often playing the devil's advocate in their interactions with teachers to help them expand their teaching horizons. As the century moves toward a close, the principal is once again the one person who can bring the school's diverse stakeholders together for the benefit of students.

Instructional leadership is "the principal's role in providing direction, resources and support to teachers and students for the improvement of teaching and learning in the school" (Keefe and Jenkins, 1984, 1991, p. vii). The role may be conceptualized in four broad domains: formative, planning, implementation and evaluation.

(1) Formative: Knowledge forms the base on which the principal builds integrity and respect. An effective instructional leader

knows the trends in school curriculum, knows various approaches to organizing schools and knows how to integrate all elements of instruction to match the learning needs of individual students.

(2) *Planning*: Instructional planning means working with teachers and other school stakeholders to develop a school design statement which includes the school's mission, psychological, philosophical and organizational assumptions and four to six essential outcomes for all learners. The statements from these three basic components have direct impact on the nine systems components (curriculum; instructional techniques; school structure and organization; school culture and climate; school leadership; management and budget; school staffing and staff development; school resources, physical plant and equipment; and evaluation plans). See First Steps, Chapter 7.

(3) *Implementation*: As instructional leader, the principal works directly with teachers in teams or individually to diagnose instructional problem areas and hypothesize solutions. He or she may teach students in a classroom or team setting and challenge teachers to look for ways to enhance the learning environment. The basis for decision making is broadened to include as many people as is reasonably possible. Responsibility is delegated to the persons best equipped to handle a situation.

(4) *Evaluation*: The principal helps everyone reflect on his or her practice. Every high school houses a wealth of data that when marshaled enables the school professionals to look more carefully at their successes and failures. The societal climate for schools will no longer tolerate fuzzy thinking and glittering generalities to support school programs. The design for any new program should contain within it a way to judge its effectiveness including the specific data to be used. It is the principal as instructional leader who establishes an example for all other professionals. "No other school official carries this responsibility so centrally, neighborhood by neighborhood across the land" (*National Commission for the Principalship*, 1990, p. 11).

THE FACILITIES MAKE A DIFFERENCE

The egg crate structures that have dominated the high school landscape for so many years are still very much with us. I vividly remember being asked to visit a newly constructed high school in Florida. The principal proudly took me around the facility room by room showing me the Spanish motif architecture and the closed circuit television system. What struck me during the tour was the similarity in this structure, which cost taxpayers millions of dollars, and the high school facilities of a previous era. What I saw on the tour were: classrooms next to classrooms; desks facing front; teachers as the focus of attention; students passively listening, or not listening as the case may be; and the library-media center absent of students. Yes, the building was modern; the architecture was beautiful, but the flexibility for helping students to activate their learning was clearly missing. Like the older, traditional buildings, the flexibility inherent in this newly constructed high school was a challenge to the creativity of the faculty.

Albert Einstein once said, "No problem can be solved from the same consciousness that created it. We must learn to see the world anew." His advice seems apropos to the facilities problem facing the bulk of high school educators desirous of reforming their schools but restricted by buildings that were designed to support a different educational program and more traditional approaches to instruction. If we educators allow ourselves to be frozen in time by the status of our buildings, then we can never bring about the kind of high school reform which each student needs to achieve optimally. The plight reminds me of a first year teacher in a high school where I was principal who noted that if only his students were motivated he could teach them effectively. I reminded him that if the students were as motivated to learn biology as he hoped, perhaps they wouldn't need him. It was his task to help them see value in what he asked them to learn.

The buildings are a given. Yes, they can be remodeled, but often if change has to wait until the building is remodeled it may be too late. The inquiry must begin with how can we change our school program to enable all students to learn effectively and use the facilities we currently have. As a start, classrooms don't have to have desks facing forward. Desks can be rearranged to facilitate the desired learning. Figure 5.3 shows a sample of a room redesign to accommodate different student activities to adjust to different learning styles. The classroom space allows for individual work, small group activities, teacher-directed instruction, an area for students who need more supervision, an informal area furnished with comfortable furniture, formal work spaces with tables and student desks and separate bright and dim light

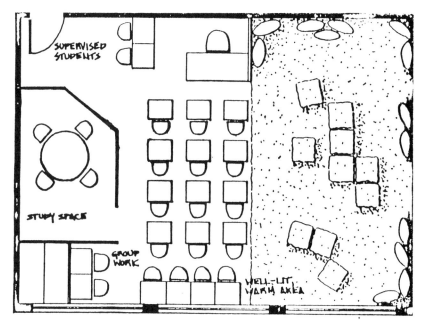

Figure 5.3. A Sample Classroom Rearranged to Accommodate Learning Style Differences.

areas. The classroom design enables teachers to adjust instructional activities to individual student learning style differences.

Teams of teachers can be scheduled in classrooms located in a common area so that students might move easily into different rooms focused on different activities. The teachers would be in close proximity to facilitate working together. Educators in one high school, desirous of having all teachers working more closely together, created one large planning area to house all the teachers. The area was landscaped so that each teacher had some privacy, as well as ample opportunity to work together. The principal's office was moved to the planning area so that she or he could be closer to the faculty.

The point of all this is that there is no "magic bullet." As principals, teachers, parents and students begin to restructure a high school program toward a constructivist approach to learning, the facilities, as one of the components, must be restructured to accommodate the anticipated changes. Certainly, existing structures and capital outlay shortfalls may prove confining, but they should not be construed as serious obstacles to change. The only serious obstacles are in our inability to dream large enough dreams.

First Steps

Step One

Enumerate the courses in the high school that have a multiaged student enrollment. Mathematics courses often have students of different stages. Band has already been mentioned. Athletic teams are composed of students with the ability to play at a given level regardless of age. Ask: Why are students of different ages able to work together successfully in these programs? What is the basis for enrollment or selection? Would a similar arrangement work for other areas of the curriculum, e.g., English, social studies, science? On what criteria should enrollment in each of these subject areas be based?

Step Two

Investigate books which describe nongraded programs either in theory or practically. Brown's *The Nongraded High School* (1963) describes one high school's approach. Buffie and Jenkins's *Curriculum Development in Nongraded Schools* (1971) presents various secondary school approaches to changing the curriculum to permit individual student progress. A new book by Robert Anderson and Barbara Pavan (1993), *Nongradedness: Helping It to Happen*, offers an excellent rationale for nongrading schools, K–12.

Step Three

Investigate the College Board Advanced Placement Program. This program is based on the belief that some high school students are ready for college level work while still in high school. Generalizing the idea of advanced placement to the entire school program results in a nongraded high school.

Step Four

Establish an interested group of English, social studies and/or science teachers to begin to examine ways to recast the curriculum in a different format to allow students to move more rapidly or slowly. Once completed, pilot the project in one or more classrooms. As the programs succeed over time, communicate the results and the process to other teachers.

Step Five

If the high school has a homeroom program, do a feasibility study of changing this program into a teacher-adviser program. Invite a teacher from a high school with an advisement program to come to the school and talk about what it means to be an adviser, and how the role of the adviser enables high schools to work more closely with individual students. Investigate some of the research findings which show that when high schools implement an advisement program that there are fewer discipline problems and dropouts are reduced (see *Teachers-as-Advisers Evaluation Reports*, Jenkins, Florida State Department of Education, 1985–1990).

Step Six

Begin to refer to departments as teams. Change the title of the department chair to team leader. Involve the teams in planning curricula for their areas and for the school. Have the teams take twenty to thirty minutes each and report at a faculty meeting what they are doing and what they are planning to do.

Step Seven

As various new programs develop look for ways to rethink the use different facilities. Ask two or three teachers to redesign their classrooms to better accommodate individual student learning styles. Ask parents for donations of furniture which could be used to establish an informal corner in each room. Add carrels where possible. Include computer stations where students can work alone or in pairs. Provide headsets for students who study best when listening to soft music. Again, have the teachers communicate their successes to other faculty members. Encourage visitations.

CHAPTER 6

Professionalizing the Role of the Teacher

Teaching is a very hard job that needs ample compensation and considerable on-the-job training for the lifetime of the teacher. Less than this will not suffice.—*William Glasser, M.D.*

TEACHING IS LIKELY the most difficult of all the professions. No job is more important to the survival of our society and the continuance of our standard of living. The abilities to solve complex problems, think analytically and generate new knowledge are critical for all persons entering the labor force in the twenty-first century. The task of preparing an expanding divergent student population falls to the institution of the schools and the primary players in those institutions, the teachers. The demands on teachers will hardly lessen as youth must prepare for a new wave of contingencies.

These demands are exacerbated by an increasingly diverse student population, which has led demographer Harold Hodgkinson to predict that by the year 2015 the present minority and majority students will change places. The present minority students are precisely the students for whom traditional education has not been effective. Moreover, he discovered that, of every 100 children born today, twelve will be born out of wedlock; forty will be born to parents who will divorce before the child is eighteen; five will be born to parents who separate; two will be born to parents one of whom will die before the child is eighteen; and forty-one will reach eighteen normally. Additionally, 50 percent of the children born out of wedlock are born to teenage mothers, which is at least twice the rate likely to occur in other nations (Hodgkinson, 1985).

The ability to cope with the new contingencies is hardly a part of the preservice training of many high school teachers. In fact few, if any, have had much grounding in how students learn. The ability to diagnose salient characteristics and match instruction to those differences are skills that must be taught on the run. When one compares the workday of a typical high school teacher with the workday of a community college instructor or university professor, there are glaring differences. Higher education speaks of teaching, research and service, all critical domains for expanding one's knowledge and skill base. High school teachers rarely have time to catch their collective breaths, let alone explore the infinite levels of content in their teaching fields or new approaches to pedagogy. How then can high schools be expected to transform themselves from places to do time to communities of learning? The answer lies in professionalizing the role of the teacher.

LEAD MANAGEMENT VERSUS BOSS MANAGEMENT

In applying the management theories of the late W. Edwards Deming to education, the psychiatrist William Glasser (1992) writes about the differences between two kinds of management, lead management and boss management. He sees teachers as managers of classrooms and students as workers. He contends that if high school students are ever going to accomplish quality work, it can only be done with a new type of management. The old boss management system limits the quality of the work and the productivity of the workers. Lead management communicates a vision of quality and runs the system so that the workers realize that it is to their advantage to do quality work. In essence teachers who boss-manage rely on coercion and other negatives to attempt to get students to work. Teachers who use lead management techniques enlist input from the students to improve the nature of curriculum and instruction and remove barriers to motivation. They devote time and energy to building programs focused on intrinsic motivation.

The two types of management apply equally to school administrators. How a school is managed provides a model for teachers as they work with students. Getting teachers to do quality work is the task of the principal and his assistants. Principals who practice lead management remove obstacles for teachers and provide resources to help them do a better job. In a lead management school the principal fixes everyone's attention on quality and helps teachers do their job. They believe in the Latin prayer *Ne Sim Obex* (may I not be an obstacle).

Table 6.1. Differences between Lead Managers and Boss Managers.

Boss Management	Lead Management
Sets the task and standards for what the workers are to do	Engages the workers in discussions of the quality of the work to be done and the time needed to do it
Tells rather than shows the workers what is to be done	Shows or models the job to be done
Inspects or grades the work or has someone else do it	Asks the workers to inspect and evaluate their own work
When workers resist, uses coercion	Provides the best tools and work spaces
Workers and managers are adversaries	Creates a nonadversarial, noncoercive atmosphere

Table 6.1 is adapted from Glasser's *The Quality School* and compares lead managers with boss managers on several key dimensions.

It is lead management in teachers that creates learning environments for students where they can progressively explore the complexities of knowing. It is lead management in principals that provides a school schedule and accompanying resources for teachers to push the limits of their knowledge. It is lead management collectively that acknowledges the importance of each person's contribution to fulfilling the school's mission.

EXPANDING COLLABORATION

In most, if not all, American high schools teaching and learning take place in isolation. Little collaboration among teachers and between teachers and administrators occurs. Teaching is often a solo activity, confined to a 750 to 900 square foot classroom behind closed doors. Effective teachers gain their reputations indirectly by word of mouth. Rarely are they observed by their colleagues working directly with students. Yet much research provides evidence of the value of collaboration in the planning of instruction. In the constructivist sense teachers need to try out their ideas in the arena of discourse with their fellow teachers. Unfortunately, the way in which high schools are organized rarely allows for such interaction.

Collaboration in a restructured high school can take many forms.

The departmental structure characteristic of most, if not all, high schools can be reconceptualized so that teachers are seen as members of a team working for the improvement of teaching and learning. These teams can meet on a regular basis with agendas focused on the inter-relationship of curriculum, instruction and assessment. The subject area teams can establish consistent standards and expectations for students and model the value of teamwork. In some cases the discipline-based team might examine ways to integrate subjects within the discipline. For example, teaching earth science, biology, chemistry and physics each year in a coordinated manner could be a project of a high school science team. Another team might consider reducing the number of units or topics to be covered to allow for learning in greater depth.

Interdisciplinary collaboration is another possibility. An interdisciplinary structure might establish three or four departments, rather than eight or nine. Again, these departments would be reconceptualized as teams working together to integrate content as appropriate. Interdisciplinary units could be developed when appropriate. When not appropriate, curriculum would be offered within the specific disciplines represented in the interdisciplinary team. In a high school with an interdisciplinary team structure, teachers are both specialists and generalists. As specialists, they bring the perspective of their disciplines to bear upon curriculum and instruction. As generalists, they stand back from their respective areas to look for ways to integrate the content of two, three or even more disciplines. When the curriculum is reformed in terms of student performances, cooperation among subject specialists is facilitated.

Other variations on collaboration are possible when teachers join inquiry teams to solve a school problem or to improve their pedagogical skills. These teams focus on the interests of teachers and usually exist for a finite period of time. Problem-centered teams are disbanded after a solution is offered. Professional development may extend over a year or beyond, depending on the nature of the subject. These teams can be extended to include parents, community experts or university professors. New technology enhances the possibility that external consultants can be enlisted to help from any place on the globe. The idea of national and international teams is still in its formative stages.

Collaboration can also involve teachers with students. Teams of teachers and students could attack a community problem. Such an approach would permit students to work side-by-side with their teachers applying knowledge to a specific problem. Several obvious benefits might accrue from this arrangement. Teachers can model problem-solving behavior. Students can observe the application of knowledge in the context of the real world. Teachers and students can generate a camaraderie which transcends the traditional teacher-student relationship. Both groups would benefit from the exchange of ideas and perspectives in constructing new meanings for content, knowledge and skills.

NEW ROLES FOR TEACHERS

Advisement

In a high school committed to a constructivist approach, two new roles for teachers and administrators emerge. The first, though not exactly new, places each professional as an adviser to a prescribed number of students. When each student has an adult friend who cares about him, the traditional factory model school environment is replaced by a culture of caring. Advisers are the significant people in the school lives of their advisees. They schedule individual conferences on a regular basis. They help construct the daily schedule for each advisee and monitor attendance and progress. They participate in course selection and help create an individual work plan for each advisee.

Advisers work closely with other faculty and staff so as to provide cogent information to impact instruction. If an advisee is not progressing well in one or two academic areas, she or he meets with the teacher(s) to discuss possible strategies. Reviewing an advisee's cognitive-learning style profile provides insights into how to present information more effectively or how to structure assignments or what cognitive skills need augmentation.

Advisement is most effective when all the professionals in the high school participate in the program. It means smaller ratios of advisers to advisees. Counselors work closely with a finite number of advisers to provide resources and help. Close communication between the counselor and the adviser means that a student can receive the help he or she needs in a timely manner.

Webster's *New World Dictionary* states that advise "implies the making of recommendations as to a course of action by someone with actual or supposed knowledge and experience." Giving advice to students requires two additional requisites: (1) the time in which to do it, and (2) a commitment on the part of the nominal school leadership to value advisers meeting one-on-one with their advisees at the expense of homerooms or advisory group meetings.

Parent involvement is another critical dimension in advancing student achievement. Sparse parent involvement is usually the rule in a traditional high school. Advisers become an important link between home and school. They take the initiative for contacting parents early in the school year and maintain the contact through conferences, telephone calls and personal notes. Sometimes, this outreach takes the form of home visits and sometimes it involves scheduling small group meetings in the community away from the school. The message sent to parents in a variety of ways is that we value your help and your involvement. You are the persons who know your son or daughter best, and we want your input.

Advisers help advisees see the connection between what they learn in school and the improvement in the quality of their lives. By being a significant person in the lives of each advisee, the adviser establishes a relationship of trust so that advisees are more likely to share less sophisticated understandings and naive conceptualizations of content. Getting this information out into the open is a critical step in moving students to more sophisticated understandings.

Research

The second new role for high school teachers had its origins in the work of Stephen M. Corey. As Director of the Horace Mann Lincoln Institute of School Experimentation, Teachers College, Columbia University, he wrote *Action Research to Improve School Practices* (1953), which described techniques to help classroom teachers examine their practices more reflectively. It was Corey's belief that the chasm between educational research and practice could be reduced when teachers engaged in a form of classroom research aimed at improving their daily practices and their professional decision making. It is a practice he labeled action research to distinguish it from more formal research practices. He cautioned, however, that action research had its limitations, but compared with the less than systematic efforts found in most schools, it was a definite improvement of the decision-making process.

All research involves accumulating and interpreting evidence, but action research focuses on evidence that helps practitioners determine whether their actions result in desirable consequences. In Corey's thinking, action research had two aspects: (1) a desirable goal and (2) an action for achieving the goal (Corey, 1953). These ingredients appear as valid today as they did over forty years ago. Today's climate for school improvement seems a natural setting for a resurgence of the notion that teachers individually and collectively can improve education at the school level.

Action research comes in two forms—quantitative and qualitative. Each has its place in the school improvement efforts. Quantitative action research uses a process of collecting facts so that the relationship of one set of facts to another can be studied. Techniques are used to produce quantified results, and if possible, generalizable conclusions. This is the type of action research that Corey described. He did caution, however, the danger in generalizing the results too far.

Qualitative research is more concerned with the individual's perceptions of the world and tends to be more subjective in its approach. Carefully written descriptions of the research setting and participants are employed in an effort to transport the consumer to the actual place and time. The quantitative researcher uses surveys, observational notes, photographs, interviews, video and audio tapes, maps of the instructional areas and journals to answer key questions. Sample questions for a qualitative research project are as follows: How can we make parent's help with homework more productive? How can we change the methods of student assessment so that they are more contextually oriented? How does teaching to student learning styles affect student achievement and attitude? What is the best way to teach higher-order thinking skills?

Action research is an outgrowth of a change process which begins with a genuine desire to improve a situation; it emanates from a feeling of dissatisfaction with a perceived disparity between aspirations and achievements. A teacher may be dissatisfied with the level of the academic progress a group of students is experiencing. A school-community may be concerned about the number of minority students referred for disciplinary action or the rate of student dropouts. A careful assessment of the status quo and an examination of the feasibility of the aspirations are then completed; this is followed by a diagnosis to determine the reasons for the aspiration-achievement disparity.

The search for promising actions that might reduce or eliminate the disparity is next conducted. The action is then carried out. Data are collected, assessments are made, and generalizations are considered. The interest is not so much in generalizing the findings, but rather in changing the behavior of the teacher(s) or in changing the practices in a given instructional area. This process can be done solo, in pairs or in teams. It requires well-planned staff development.

Two high school English teachers conducted an action research project to determine the impact of multiage classes on the students' ability to handle emotionally challenging material. They were concerned that when the age range in their classes was from fifteen to eighteen that the younger students were not mature enough to deal with difficult content. Much to their surprise, they found the students displayed little reluctance in discussing the most challenging of topics. It led one of the teachers to conclude, "If Booth Tarkington had written *Seventeen* in 1995, he would have to call it *Twelve.*"

Action research at its best is ongoing. The answer to one question may lead to several others, and the depth of the new question(s) is inextricably related to the quality of the answer to the previous one. As the novice teacher-researcher moves along the developmental continuum toward mastery of the action research process, his or her professional behavior is impacted positively. He or she becomes increasingly more in control of the teaching-learning process and more of a generator of knowledge than a consumer.

In a high school committed to the constructivist approach to learning, action research seems a logical inclusion. Teachers, administrators and students are all part of a community of learning. The difference is simply a matter of maturity, knowledge and experience. When teachers examine their own practices, they model a value for learning and a process of inquiry for their students. When teachers and administrators work togehter to solve school problems in a systematic manner, they learn from each other. When teachers directly investigate new ways to teach and new ways to organize for instruction, they gain more control of the school improvement process.

If the education of high school students is best served through a constant search for better ways to teach and to learn, then no practice, no matter how vested, is considered hallowed. Even the most stable practices should be open to modification or replacement if better ways can be discovered. A major goal of every high school in America should be the search for more effective educational practices to enhance the opportunities for learning for all students. This continuous search and implementation can bring with it an ever-spiraling "Hawthorne Effect." Each step becomes a means rather than an end. As one practice is implemented, a search to make it obsolete is begun.

FINDING SUPPORT FOR GROWTH

Both advisement and research take time. Effective advisement requires about five hours per week on the average. Conducting research takes even longer. In the case of the latter, however, the topic is often integrated into the ongoing instructional process. In a high school where personalized education is emphasized, individual scheduling holds as much for teachers as it does for students. No longer is a teacher's responsibility defined as five classes a day and 750 student contacts per week. Flexibility for students and teachers is the rule.

Organizing into teams enables teachers to teach to their strengths—content and pedagogical. For example, lectures and presentations to students should be done by teachers who are able to make content literally come alive for students. Seminars and small group discussions should be led by teachers who can craft penetrating questions, often spontaneously, to challenge students to think beyond their present level of understanding. Coaching and tutorials should be done by teachers who are effective working one-on-one or one-on-two with students. Like students, teachers have a learning style that, when accommodated, facilitates improved performance to enhance their contribution to the school and benefit students.

How a high school is staffed can provide teachers with important professional time to advise, conduct research, write curriculum and plan instruction. The requirement to carry the "bedpans" of teaching can be shifted from the professional staff to others. Differentiated staffing patterns can include instructional assistants with two years of college in an academic major, clerical aides and general aides. Instructional aides work directly with students, supervising independent study and leading small group discussions. Clerical aides maintain records, duplicate materials and distribute materials to students. General aides supervise the cafeteria, the bus ramps, and the hallways, arrange lab materials in subjects such as science and art, and distribute audio-visual equipment throughout the school. All of these tasks are important to the operation of the high school and can be done effectively by staff members other than teachers.

Technology can reduce the paperwork for teachers. It can also offer interactive instructional options where no teachers are needed. Students can work at home for part of the school day, accessing information via modems or writing papers on their personal computers. Community services can be enlisted to help teach physical fitness, instrumental music and dance. Community-based mentors can work with students in cognitive apprenticeships. The creation of professional development schools can bring larger numbers of preservice teachers from colleges of education to high school centers. Volunteer programs can be organized to bring the elderly from their homes or retirement villages to the school for periods of time each week. The possibilities seem endless. What is required is a new vision on the part of lead managers and a commitment to rethink the budgetary process.

Professionalization of the role of the teacher in a school dedicated to constructivism calls for at least one additional ingredient. Teachers must be helped to evaluate their own work. The process of administrators observing teachers teaching a prescribed number of times each year and then arriving at an annual evaluation may be grist for the union contract, but it hardly fits the current milieu. Self-evaluation seems a necessary requisite for moving to a constructivist approach to schooling. A generative model of teacher improvement simply makes more sense than one which places the emphasis upon a boss manager judging a teacher annually. Evaluation should be ongoing and continuous. Deming exhorted businesses and institutions to focus on the process as a means to improving the product. He believed that people are intrinsically motivated and will improve their performances when they see what they are asked to do as adding quality to their lives. Involving teachers in their own evaluation builds on the notion of intrinsic motivation and provides another important model for students.

As a starter, teacher evaluation procedures might reflect a personalized model of learning that resembles the instructional model for students. Having teachers establish the criteria for which they want to be held accountable can occur in a conference with the principal or an assistant at the beginning of an academic year. These criteria should be based upon the previous year's work as it relates to the long-term teaching and career goals of the individual teacher. The criteria would be accompanied by a plan for monitoring progress toward achievement of the plan on an ongoing basis. Whenever possible, the monitoring process should be self-monitoring. If a teacher lacks skills to accomplish this end, then the school leadership recommends appropriate training. Using portfolios and other forms of alternative assessment that are being proffered for students demonstrates value for the procedure and teaches the teacher a way to apply the approach to students.

First Steps

Step One

Distribute copies of Table 6.1 which lists Glasser's distinction between lead management and boss management. Have the teachers discuss each dimension in a small group setting and then present their perceptions to the total group. A team learning format seems to work best when presenting new information. This format provides a common experience, in this case reading, for the whole group and then asks them to break into groups of five to seven to answer specific questions about the material. The questions are written so that the first two can be answered by simply copying from the distributed material. For example, "List two ways lead management differs from boss management." The next questions, three or four, ask the participants to reflect on the content and combine what is given with information they already know. For example, "Do you agree with Dr. Glasser's premise that teachers are either boss managers or lead managers? Why or why not?" "Give some specific examples of teacher behavior that can be classified under one of the dimensions of lead management." Finally, the participants are asked to use the material in a creative way. For example, "Role play an example of a boss manager teacher." "Role play a lead manager teacher." "Write a limerick which contrasts boss management and lead management." The added value of this activity is that it applies to teachers a technique that they can add to their teaching repertoires for application to students at a later time.

Step Two

Change the departmental structure to a team structure and rename the department chair team leader (see First Steps of Chapter 5).

Step Three

Provide appropriate staff development to help teachers learn about the advisement role. When all members of the professional staff serve as advisers, it helps teachers to see the value of the new role (again, see First Steps, Chapter 5).

Step Four

Work with a local university if possible to offer staff development on the concept of action research. The course could be offered on a voluntary basis for graduate credit. The teachers would be taught to do action research in a school setting. Projects could be done singly or in pairs and would focus on a question that they have about their own teaching situation. The staff development meetings would focus on the procedures for completing an action research project. The university consultant would work with each project, meeting with the teachers on an individual or pair basis to help them formulate a question, review the salient literature and conduct the study. Inasmuch as this workshop might be the first experience that teachers have had with action research, it is imperative that they have a measure of success. The skill of the consultant is critical to helping the teachers limit their projects to what is possible given their work loads.

Step Five

Request permission to pilot a new approach to teacher evaluation as described in the chapter. Ostensibly, the approach might involve a few teachers at first. A number of school districts are investigating the use of more personalized approaches to teacher evaluation. Teachers determine their own goals in concert with the administrator of record and then identify ways to assess their attainment. Portfolios are one option. Monitoring teacher progress toward the achievement of their goals is similar to the behavior that teachers are asked to do as advisers for their advisees.

CHAPTER 7

Taking Charge of Time

Ordinary people think merely how they spend their time; a man of intellect tries to use it.—*Arthur Schopenhauer, 1788–1860*

THE SCHEDULE, PROBABLY more than any other one entity, controls the activities of the high school. What students do, when they do it and with whom are all questions which have their answer in the school schedule. Despite periodic complaints about the length of the school year and rigidity of the daily schedule, not much has changed in the past 100 years. The high school schedule is still a product of the factory model and the school year still reflects an agrarian mind-set. Even more basic, the division of time into convenient modules dates back to Aristotelian logic and the Western bias of separating subjects from objects (English, 1993).

Westerners think in terms of accomplishing tasks in a sequential order. The East views time as polychromatic, meaning many things happen at once. This different view of time can be instructive for Western educators who wish to shift the control of the learning process to the students and teachers (English, 1993). Such a shift appears consistent with the notions of constructivism which describes reality as an individual creation. The implication for school scheduling places control of the enterprise closer to where the learning is to occur, namely, the student and the teacher.

The 1960s brought a search for high school schedules that would offer more options for teachers and students. There was much interest in flexible scheduling. Modular schedules were attempted in some high schools to provide different time frames for different school activities.

91

It was reasoned that some activities need longer than the fifty to fifty-five minute periods, and some activities did not require as much time. Instead, high schools adopted a fifteen or twenty minutes module which extended the six or seven period day to twelve, eighteen or twenty-four. Classes were often scheduled for a different number of modules on different days of the week.

Some schedules allowed for large group, small group and independent study activities. In the NASSP Model Schools Project students were scheduled into large group motivational sessions and follow-up small group discussions in each of eight or nine subject areas on a regular cycle, usually every two weeks. In between, the students worked independently under the direction of a teacher or team of teachers to complete learning guides. In this arrangement much of the student's week was devoted to independent pursuits. More conventional scheduling was provided for students who needed more structure. In a few schools daily-demand scheduling attempted to personalize the learning process even further.

Unfortunately, in many cases once the flexible time arrangement was in place, it too developed a kind of rigidity. Modular schedules had repeating A and B weeks. Large group instruction sessions became immutable, and teachers struggled to create exciting things to do to get students "turned on" to the subject matter. The daily-demand schedule required a teacher adviser system to guide students with appropriate choices and to monitor student progress. It was frequently too cumbersome to control.

PRESENT EFFORTS TO CHANGE THE SCHOOL SCHEDULE

Today, with the drive to restructure the high school, there is a renewed interest in school scheduling. Several "new" approaches are available for study and implementation. One such approach with an intriguing label is the *Copernican Plan*. This plan is the brainchild of Dr. Joseph Carroll, a former school superintendent in New Mexico and Massachusetts. It is Carroll's contention that the Carnegie unit with its time constraints is the real enemy of meaningful teaching and learning. He cites remedial summer programs as examples of improved learning when students can focus on one or two subjects for longer periods of time (Carroll, 1994). This notion undergirds Copernican scheduling. Students take fewer subjects for longer periods of time for only part of the school year. For example, students meet in classes for blocks of time (90 minutes, 120 minutes, 240 minutes) each day. It is surmised that students can focus better and more in depth when fewer classes are taken. Teachers have fewer preparations and fewer students to get to know at any one time. They also must rethink the use of time since the longer block does not lend itself to traditional lecture-centered teaching.

A number of high schools are experimenting with block scheduling where students meet periods one, three and five on Mondays and Wednesdays and periods two, four and six on Tuesdays and Thursdays. On Friday they meet all six classes. Meeting three classes four days per week allows for more time to be devoted to the study of subjects similar to what occurs at the university level. The double blocks of time are for all subjects regardless of special circumstances. Teachers are encouraged to undertake different approaches to instruction during the longer periods.

Somewhat similar to this schedule is one that offers a seven period day on a rotational basis and doubles one class period per week. During a typical week each class meets for the same number of minutes but does not meet each day. By rotating each class period through the schedule each student with different learning style preferences for time of day can be accommodated partially. Again the double class meeting provides time for teachers and students to plan different activities. Figure 7.1 is an example of the rotational schedule.

A popular approach to block scheduling uses a four by four model where students enroll in four courses each semester. By extending each class period to eighty-five to ninety-five minutes students are able to

Monday	Tuesday	Wednesday	Thursday	Friday
1	7	6	5	3
2	1	7	6	5
2	1	7	6	5
3	2	1	7	6
4	4	4	4	4
5	3	2	3	7
6	3	5	2	1
*Period 4 = lunch				

Figure 7.1. A Rotational Schedule with One Double Period.

```
          7:55- 9:10—Period one
          9:15-10:40—Period two
         10:45-11:40—Period three, lunch
         11:45- 1:10—Period four
          1:15- 2:40—Period five
```

Figure 7.2. A Block Schedule with a Lunch, Activities and Study Hall Period.

finish a year's work in a semester and complete eight courses per year. Two variations of the four by four schedule are shown in Figures 7.2 and 7.3.

Another variation comes from the Coalition of Essential Schools. Here high school organization is guided by nine common principles. One of the principles calls for tailoring the school practices to meet the needs of every group or class of adolescents. This can hardly be accomplished using traditional scheduling. Additionally, a second principle calls for personalizing education to the maximum possible extent. Purposely, the Coalition does not prescribe what member schools should do or not do. It only provides the nine general principles and then leaves implementation strategies to the building level educators. Yet, in his book *Horace's School: Redesigning the American High School,* Sizer (1992) includes a sample schedule for the mythical Franklin High School.

The school for 1350 students is organized into five houses with thirteen teachers and 270 students each. Each house has a schedule. In the example given, periods one, two and six are one hour and forty-five minutes each. Periods three, four and five share two hours, which are used for lunch, advisement and tutorials. Classes rotate through the periods one, two and six to provide the opportunity for teachers and students to meet at different times during the day. Special periods before and after school are arranged for band, chorus and similar ac-

```
          8:15- 9:45—Period one
          9:55-11:25—Period two
         11:30-12:15—Lunch
         12:20- 1:50—Period three
          2:00- 3:30—Period four
```

Figure 7.3. A Block Schedule with a Common Lunch Period.

tivities. A team meeting is scheduled each day (Sizer, 1992). Common planning time can also be provided by scheduling a half day of each student's week for community service. The seventy students on each team would perform community and school service at the same time. This would give the team a chance to plan for three uninterrupted hours per week on company time.

GUIDELINES FOR SCHEDULING

Regardless of the scheduling configuration, care must be taken initially to be very clear on what the schedule is attempting to accomplish. A schedule is a tool, not something which stands by itself. The decision to schedule a school one way as opposed to another should be integrated with the overall philosophy, goals and objectives of the school community.

Given the differences within and among high schools, schedules may differ. Educators must keep in mind, however, that the nature of the schedule facilitates the teaching and learning process. In a school dedicated to the constructivist approach certain principles should drive the creation of the schedule. A list of these principles would include the following:

(*1*) Learning is an individual matter. Insofar as possible each student works with content and activities commensurate with his or her background and interest.

(*2*) The walls of the school should join the school with the community. Community learning is an integral part of the school curriculum.

(*3*) Opportunities to work independently and in learning teams should be part of the school program.

(*4*) Students should complete their work in the best setting for the work to be completed – school, home, and community all qualify as learning centers.

(*5*) Time on task is related to the intrinsic motivation that the students bring to the learning activity. The length of learning modules should be flexible to accommodate individual differences.

(*6*) Students should spend time with advisers in determining what to do and when to do it.

(*7*) Students who need strengthening in learning how to learn should be provided with regular instruction in the appropriate areas.

(8) Sufficient time should be provided to allow students to complete in-depth learning tasks.

(9) The Carnegie unit can be adjusted to fit most any circumstance and is open to various definitions and interpretations.

A LEARNER-DRIVEN SCHOOL SCHEDULE

The ideal schedule would seem to adapt to the individual needs of each learner. At first glance such an undertaking seems out of the realm of possibility for the typical high school. It raises questions of control, responsibility and structure. Simply keeping track of individual students daily would seem an overwhelming task, and may require more expenditure of human energy than the benefits accrued. Yet, given the nature of learning and the increasing diversity of high school student bodies, it may be the only sensible next step. New discoveries in the cognitive sciences further reinforce the need to rethink how students and teachers spend their days at school.

A high school schedule that focuses on individual learners shifts the major responsibility for learning from the adults to the students. While full implementation of this ideal might be a distant vision, steps toward its attainment are not. In fact several of the proposed schedules presented earlier in this chapter can be viewed as initial steps. With the present sophistication in computer technology, it is possible to envision a personalized schedule for each student, which accounts for time spent and progress made.

Considerable progress has been made in several schools over the past twenty years to develop personalized school schedules. These efforts are meshed with other activities and programs to make the traditional master schedule unnecessary. Placing students in classrooms for uniform periods of time to receive similar instruction appears out of touch with the times in which we live. What then is a suitable alternative? How does a high school develop a schedule based on individual need, interest, learning style and desired curriculum experiences?

Ostensibly, the personalized school schedule begins with a blank sheet. Teachers and students then fill in the blanks by requesting times for specific activities. In some cases meetings of groups of students are necessary. Band and chorus are two such activities. Seminars to discuss important content must be scheduled. Community-based learning often requires specific time frames. Any activity that can only be accomplished by a group or whose objectives are better achieved by meeting in groups should be placed on the blank schedule. Some of the group meetings are ongoing while others are transitory in nature.

Minimally, two ingredients are critical to the development of a personalized schedule for each student. Students need advisers to help them make appropriate choices. It is the adviser who meets with the student on a regular basis to facilitate decisions as to where a student should spend time during the day. Usually, the adviser meets with the advisees at the beginning of each day to establish the personalized schedule. In some cases the schedule can be developed for a week at a time with daily changes made as needed.

The second ingredient is the nature of the curriculum and the instructional delivery system. Obviously, state and district curriculum mandates must be acknowledged such as graduation requirements, length of school day and minutes per subject per week. Waiver processes are now in effect in many states, which give some latitude in implementing these requirements. When possible, curriculum requirements should be made flexible to allow opportunities for student choices. Once a decision is made as to what is required and what is optional curricula, a personalized system of instruction can be implemented. There are essentially two directions this can take.

The first builds on previous efforts at continuous progress learning. In this system, objectives for each course are identified. Units of instruction are developed around clusters of objectives and materials, which permit students to work at their own pace. When they successfully complete all the units associated with a particular course, they receive credit and move on to the next course in sequence. For example, the successful completion of Algebra I leads students to Algebra II or geometry. Pretests determine initial placement in the sequences. Criterion-referenced posttests determine the readiness to advance to the next unit. Students schedule themselves into testing centers when they are ready to take a posttest. Figure 7.4 shows how a course can be constructed for continuous progress learning.

The course is divided into units with specific objectives related to the overall course objectives. Learning guides are developed by teachers to enable students to meet the unit and course objectives. The guides may differ but usually follow a common format. They begin with an introductory paragraph which provides the students with an overview. The introduction is followed by the outcomes students can be expected to

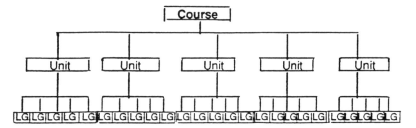

Figure 7.4. A Schematic Design for Creating a Continuous Progress Course.

attain upon completing the guide. How the students will be evaluated follows the outcomes. The evaluation section gives students a description of what they must complete and to what standard in order to complete the guide successfully. A section describing the resources to be used in the guide is next. Learning activities and an activity completion checklist conclude the guide.

The learning activities lead the students to textbooks, outside reading, interactive videos, hands-on materials, field trips, community-based experiences, seminars, experiments, computer activities, skill shops and a variety of other activities intended to help students reach the objectives of the guide. Insofar as possible, activities are designed to accommodate individual student learning styles and intellectual levels. Commercially developed materials may be used as supplements or alternatives to the learning guides. Obviously, any commercial materials must be integrated appropriately into the overall scheme of the continuous progress learning system.

Contracting is another way to personalize the learning process. Here, students and teachers design their own learning environments. Like the learning guides format above, the contracts include objectives, activities and a method of evaluation. In addition, a completion schedule is developed to establish deadlines and to monitor progress. The contract allows for attention to be given to a student's individual needs and interests. The format for a contract may vary, but it typically contains specific elements to guide the student's work. A directions section describes how the contract will be completed. A content section identifies a subject/topic to be covered, clear statements of objectives, activities to meet the objectives, a list of resources to be used, a time line with due dates and a method of evaluation. A signatures section provides a place for the student, teacher, parent(s) and other adults to sign (see Chapter 9 for an example of a contract form).

Contract learning may be used in parallel with the continuous progress format or separately. In some cases contracts may be integrated into learning guides to offer students opportunities to branch out into areas of individual interest. Because contract learning places major responsibility for learning upon the students, it requires systematic student training. Some students are more ready than others to undertake contracts. Consequently, establishing a procedure for gradually increasing student input seems wise. For example, initially, the teacher may take more responsibility for selecting and organizing content, developing activities and establishing due dates. As students demonstrate their ability to create their own structures, they should be allowed to do so. The process calls for teacher sensitivity to the different ways in which students learn. While providing some structure is probably necessary for all students, some students require more than others.

In a high school organized by contract learning, students contract to complete various parts of a course. Defining course expectations in terms of outcomes facilitates this process. Students are able to contract to complete the expectations in their own way and at their own pace. Monitoring progress is the responsibility of the student, the teacher, the parents and other adults who have signed the contract. In time, it is hoped that most students can assume increasing responsibility for their own learning. Chapter 9 shows a sample format for a student contract.

Figure 7.5 shows a sample student weekly plan form for learner-directed scheduling. This is an actual weekly schedule for a student at the Thomas Haney Secondary Centre in Maple Ridge, British Columbia.

In this schedule, some of the times are fixed, such as meetings with the adviser, self defense and choir. All other times are scheduled by the students working with the adviser. Teacher-scheduled meetings for seminars and other forms of instruction are presented on a weekly basis and given to the advisers in written form. Advisers then direct students who are affected by the meetings to place it on their schedules. The time that each student devotes to the study of a subject(s) is monitored by the adviser using a computer database. Advisers continuously monitor the academic progress of the students. With advances in technology the entire scheduling process can be managed by having students download their scheduling choices from personal laptop computers into a larger computer which would then develop common possibilities.

Monday:	
8:30–9:30	Advisement
9:30–10:30	Self defense, small gym
10:30–12:00	Choir
1:00–2:00	Start creative work for Learning Guide (LG) 12, short story
2:00–3:00	Social studies—LG 14, Activity #2. Read units and make summaries
Tuesday:	
8:45–9:30	English seminar, LG 11, Room 1127
9:30–10:30	Self defense
10:30–11:00	French "Moi"
11:00–12:00	Research #2, Room 1117 English, LG 13
1:00–2:00	Social studies, polish LG 14 to hand in
2:00–3:00	View video from social studies LG 14
Wednesday:	
8:45–10:30	French—ask to make sure all LG's are done. Study for final
10:30–12:00	Choir
1:00–2:00	English LG 5. Grammar test—testing center
2:00–3:00	Continue with LG 12, creative work
Thursday:	
8:30–9:30	Advisement
9:30–10:30	Self defense
10:30–12:00	English—read Chrysalis #1
1:00–2:00	Social studies—LG 12—work on map of lower mainland
2:00–3:00	Study for French final
Friday:	
8:30–10:30	English—LG 12, creative assignment
10:30–12:00	French final—testing center
1:00–3:00	Social studies, complete LG 15
Note:	This student schedules lunch 12:00–1:00 each day

Figure 7.5. Sample Weekly Plan for Learner-Directed Scheduling.

100

REDEFINING THE CARNEGIE UNIT

The Carnegie unit has been a part of the American high school scene for almost a century. It was begun in 1907 in response to college's need for high schools to establish a standard to assess the courses that students completed for graduation. The Carnegie Foundation for the Advancement of Teaching advocated that "14 . . . standard units of credit be required for entrance to college as evidence of substantial preparation. Each unit came to represent a minimum of about 130 instructional hours" (Maeroff, 1993). By 1931 more than 75 percent of the high schools had accepted the idea of the Carnegie unit in reporting student achievement. Today, it is even more prevalent, with virtually all student transcripts reflecting the subjects and credits completed during the years in school. The Carnegie unit directly influences the length of class periods, the length of the school day and the length of the school year. Indirectly, it influences the nature of instruction.

The proliferation of restructuring efforts have brought attention to many of the outmoded practices induced by the Carnegie unit. State and national efforts stress the superiority of determining student performance over time spent in class. In this context, the Carnegie unit is depicted as an enemy of innovative practice. Actually, the Carnegie is simply a concept that educators tend to define in a certain way. Given the history of the Carnegie unit in American education, the definition currently in use is predictable. This is not to say, however, that the current definition must remain. It only reflects an unwillingness to change in light of new information.

Rather than abolish the Carnegie unit, which has currency among parents, students and college admissions officers, perhaps it might be prudent to consider keeping the symbol and changing the meaning. Presently, Carnegie units imply number of hours in class and the level of achievement. They are reported in terms of credits, with one Carnegie unit equal to one credit. Since one is a whole number, there is no reason why it could not be reported in fractions or parts.

If courses were redefined in terms of outcomes, objectives, units or something similar and these terms were tied to fractions of a Carnegie unit, each time a student successfully completed a section, he or she would be awarded a fraction of a credit. Full course credit would be withheld until the full course was run, and the student demonstrated completion of the course outcomes. Partial credit should not be difficult to record given the state of technology.

For example, if an American history course was defined in terms of twelve major outcomes, each time students demonstrated mastery of an outcome they would receive one-twelfth of a credit. Students would continue through the course until they successfully complete all twelve outcomes. In another example when students contract to complete content in their own way, the teacher can assign partial credit to the contract so that when it is finished the partial credit can be awarded. For extended community service students might earn more than a credit.

Shifting the emphasis to performance rather than uniform time-spent appears a better way to report what a student can do. In this way the counting of hours is not primary to determining student accomplishment. What students are able to do and apply is considered of greater importance. Thus a transcript becomes a dynamic instrument which signifies what students have learned. It changes as students become more proficient.

REAL CHANGE VERSUS SYMBOLIC CHANGE

Much of the tinkering with high school schedules reflects symbolic rather than real change. Simply implementing a block schedule or dividing the school timetable into smaller units or modules accomplishes very little. The argument that block scheduling forces teachers to teach differently seems to beg the question for changing the schedule in the first place. Every high school is a system and is part of a larger system. Changes that impact student learning positively are part of a larger whole. This is why changes in the school schedule must be accompanied by changes in other parts of the school. In fact changes in the school schedule probably ought to be the last consideration.

The role of the high school teacher changes from one of presenter of information to one who sits beside students and guides them individually. Teachers assume responsibilities similar to their university colleagues as they divide their days into advisement, teaching, curriculum development and service. The school is staffed differently. Typical student teacher ratios may be increased in order to provide for paraprofessional assistance. Some aides supervise students; others distribute materials; while others maintain records and publish materials. Preservice teachers are placed in schools as aides to teachers or teams of teachers.

Variegated instruction replaces the one-size-fits-all mentality of the traditional high school. Students learn in different ways. They have different strengths and different areas in need of strengthening. Instruction is directed to student strengths. Skill shops are offered to augment skills in processing information and to strengthen basics. The size of student groups and the need for group meetings is determined by the nature of the instruction. Uniform-sized groups meeting every day are purged from the schedule with few exceptions. Locations for learning are expanded from the classroom and the school setting to the community and even the home.

The schedule is more than a mechanical means for placing students and teachers together for finite periods of time. It is primarily a philosophy of teaching and learning which places the learners at the center from which all decisions about people, program, materials and structure are made.

First Steps

Step One

Develop a school design statement which contains eleven components, three basic and eight system. The format was created by Howard and Keefe under the auspices of the National Association of Secondary School Principals (see Howard and Keefe, 1993).

BASIC COMPONENTS

(*1*) Mission Statement: Why do we exist as a school?

(*2*) Philosophical, Psychological and Organizational Assumptions: What is learning? What is the purpose of formal schooling? How should our school be organized to enable each student to succeed and do a measure of quality work?

(*3*) Student Outcomes Statement: Four to six essential outcomes for all students to participate effectively in the contingencies for the 21st century as now projected.

SYSTEM COMPONENTS

(*1*) Curriculum and Instructional Programs: Define the curriculum content and learning opportunities that will be offered.

(*2*) Instructional Techniques: Describe the various teaching techniques that are consistent with the psychological, philosophical and organizational assumptions.

(3) School Structure and Organization: This section includes descriptors of the *school schedule.*

(4) School Culture and Climate: Describe the cultural norms and traditions of the school and community. Describe the enduring characteristics of the school.

(5) School Leadership, Management and Budgeting: Describe how school planning, decision making and communication are managed.

(6) School Staffing and Staff Development: Describe the numbers of teachers, paraprofessionals, etc., required to implement the basic components. Include statements about necessary staff development.

(7) School Resources, Physical Plant and Equipment: Describe how the facilities will support the program. What changes, if any, must be made? What are the priorities?

(8) Evaluation Plan: Describe the various ways parents and the community will be involved and informed about the school plan for improvement and evidence of successes.

The point to remember in Step One is that the school schedule is a systems component of more basic decisions about teaching and learning. It grows out of and supports the school's mission and its expectations for staff and students. The formulation of the school design statement should involve representatives of stakeholder groups and be subject to open discussion and amendment. A well-defined school improvement plan might be substituted for the school design statement.

Step Two

Assuming the need for a different schedule, begin by simply doubling the traditional class periods two days per week. The total number of minutes for instruction will not be diminished, but it will give teachers and students an opportunity to work with a slightly different timetable.

Step Three

If the doubling of each class period once per week results in some success, then consider moving to a four by four model. The literature contains a number of descriptions of different variations on this theme. [See Mahaffey, 1995, *The Bulletin,* May, Reston, Virginia: National Association of Secondary School Principals or Hottenstein and

Malatesta (1993) or a new monograph by Henry Traverso (1995) published by NASSP.]

Step Four

Consider establishing a thirty-day intersession in January between the first and second semester. During the intersession the students would enroll in one course or one experience for credit. Flexibility in programming should be strongly encouraged. Extended field trips could be scheduled to distant states or countries. Students could volunteer service in the community. Community internships could be provided. Problem-oriented experiences could be tied to traditional subject areas. Interdisciplinary units might be planned. Scheduling would be determined by the teacher(s) in charge of the various programs. A minimum of three ingredients should be considered in planning such a venture: (1) Develop a carefully written plan describing what will take place and why. Involve teachers, students and parents. (2) Present the plan to the administrative hierarchy in the district and next to the school board. (3) Develop a means of evaluation and report the findings publicly.

PART FOUR

THE LEARNING ENVIRONMENT

CHAPTER 8

Managing Students More Effectively: A Different Look at Discipline

Discipline involves real-world consequences or interventions, or a combination of the two. It deals with the reality of the situation, not with the power and control of the adult.—*Barbara Coloroso (1994)*

MADOLYN HUNTER ONCE remarked how interesting it was that when times get tough people tend to invoke the worst practices which were applied to them in the process of their growing up. Maybe that's a reason why high school educators are so willing to use threats, coercion and punishment to attempt to get students under control. Over the past decade the public has identified poor student discipline as the most pressing problem facing high schools. Violence has reached a stage in some schools where resource officers and security guards are a regular part of the school staff.

Is it possible to stem the tide of violence in our high schools? What conditions would be necessary to eliminate all forms of external control so that the dollars spent on guards could be used to support learning? Is expulsion of all troublemakers the answer? Are certain students destined by genetics to become criminals, as a recent book implies (Herrnstein and Murray, 1994)? Are magnet schools a solution to the problem? Can alternative placements help ameliorate the problem?

Perhaps one answer to the problem can be found in observing kindergarten children on the first day of school. Few, if any, come expecting problems. Most children arrive on that first day with eager anticipation. School is viewed as a place of high personal quality. What happens between that eventful first day of school and the high school experience is well-documented in case study after case study of students who remove school from their personal value system, usually as a result of failure to achieve. They reason that if you can't pay your dues, then why belong to the organization? Dr. William Glasser tells the story of a trip to a junior high school in the Watts district of Los Angeles. It was sometime in the 1960s; and, he was hired by the principal to come to the school to meet with selected students. After talking individually with about eight students, Dr. Glasser asked the principal if he had any more students in the school like the eight he had just met. The principal said, "Our whole school is composed of such students." Dr. Glasser, refusing the consulting fee and expenses, announced that he was leaving to go home. Upon leaving he said to the disappointed principal, "Let me give you some advice. Don't irritate those kids."

This story has remained a part of my active memory for thirty years because it describes the problems of much student misbehavior directly and profoundly. Imbedded in the account of the visit is a summary of what's wrong with schools from the viewpoint of the students. If quality has no meaning except as defined by the customer, as Deming asserts, then the task of high school educators is to restore school as a place of quality in the lives of more students. This challenge seems clearly related to helping all students gain success in the context of their high school education.

CONTROL THEORY: WHY A DIFFERENT APPROACH CAN WORK

All human beings share a common set of genetic needs that must be met within the context of society's institutions. The family is obviously the most important institution to meeting these needs, but for a large number of students the school runs a close second. Glasser (1986) proposes that everyone, regardless of his status, is destined to satisfy five basic needs: survival, belonging, power, freedom and fun. In his book *Control Theory in the Classroom* (1986), Glasser contends that to the degree these needs are met people become relatively good and productive citizens. When the needs are frustrated, people experience pain. Over a long period of time this pain produces a lasting and debilitating effect.

When people successfully meet their basic needs, they experience pleasure and associate that pleasure with the specifics (place, people and circumstances) surrounding the experience. These places, people and experiences become a part of a person's memory as entities that have successfully satisfied a basic need or needs in the past and will likely do so in the future. They are like the pictures we place in a photograph album. They have value for us personally. These places, people and experiences become part of what Glasser labels the "quality world."

The behaviors that people choose are related to the satisfaction of one or more of the five basic needs. The behaviors they continue to choose are behaviors that in each person's mind reduces the disparity between what they want and what they have. The behaviors and their accompanying perceptions are specific and individual. In this context behavior actually controls perception (Glasser, 1981). Consequently, the key to controlling student behavior in school is to get them to behave differently so that their perception of school as a need-satisfying place changes.

The concept of behavior is a tricky one. For years we have operated high schools on the assumption that human behavior is externally controlled. This is to say, if we want students to behave in a certain way, then we need to create outside situations which force them to do so. This assumption has produced a school culture driven by punishment, fear and coercion which has worked with some students. Unfortunately, given today's culture it works for fewer and fewer students causing high schools to implement stronger and stronger measures to control students. Viewed differently, however, the key to controlling students is not to increase the external controls, but to create ways to shift the responsibility for control back to the students. From this perspective, control theory seems a logical way to organize a high school.

CONTROL THEORY APPLIED TO THE SCHOOL

Achieving order in a high school usually comes down to a debate between the hardliners and the apologists. Ninety percent or better of high school educators choose the hardline position. Threatening, criticizing, angering, yelling, detaining, suspending and expelling are all behaviors familiar to high school educators. We have been using them for decades with limited success when recidivism is used as an indicator. The students whom we see once for irresponsible acts are the students we see again and again. A minority of students demand the majority of the educator's time.

The application of control theory to the high school provides us with an idea that works. It is based on four main concepts:

(1) People are self-controlling beings who act to meet their life needs.
(2) Behavior is always a choice between alternatives. People choose the alternatives that seem to best meet the needs thay have at the moment.
(3) Experience and thinking provide people with the alternatives from which to choose their behavior. Each behavior chosen has its own consequence.
(4) People are internally controlled. They choose behaviors that will make the external world more closely coincide with the world they want. The closer the match between external and internal worlds the more satisfied people tend to be (Glasser, 1986).

In developing a discipline program that incorporates these four basic concepts, one begins with the belief that a satisfying education reduces the need for an elaborate system. If students find the high school a place that coincides with their quality worlds and satisfies their basic needs, then they are unlikely to search for less responsible ways to meet them.

The many experiences within a high school take on different meanings for different students. Students who see school as a place where most of their needs are met judge school to be a good place. Students who find school unappealing either drop out, choose a variety of irresponsible behaviors or do just enough to get by. It is to those students who choose irresponsible behavior for whom discipline programs are directed. Some of these students are students who usually have had a long history of failure, beginning in elementary school and continuing through high school. They fail to make the connection between doing what the school asks them to do and improving their lives. How then can school discipline be reorganized to address the needs of both the students who occasionally break the rules and those who frequently break them? Before we can answer that question, it is helpful to examine each of the five basic needs.

Survival refers to hunger, thirst, sexual desire and other physiological needs that are relatively distinct. Discomforts attached to the frustration of these needs are easily determined. What an individual must do to satisfy these needs is rather straightforward but not always easily achieved. Survival needs often take precedence over any of the psychological needs, but not always.

Belonging means that students feel they are a part of the high school. When students believe that someone in school cares about them and wants them to succeed, they feel they belong. People fulfill this need by sharing and cooperating with others.

Power is tied to achievement and the recognition that comes with it. When students succeed in academic classes or in student activities or both, they satisfy their need for power. If they do not succeed in these areas, they look for other ways to satisfy this need. People fulfill this need by accomplishments, by being recognized and respected and by being listened to.

Freedom means making choices. Having a say about what is done in school helps satisfy this need. Unfortunately, options are not available to all students; from first bell to last, they are told what to do. People fulfill this need by making choices in their lives.

Fun is associated with laughter, enjoyment and joy. Effective teachers make the content interesting and enjoyable. When students are learning, they will tell you they are having fun. School does not have to be drudgery; we all work harder when we enjoy what we are doing.

These five basic needs drive all human behavior. Students who satisfy these needs on a regular basis in a school setting are rarely a problem; students who do not, irritate educators who in turn irritate the students creating a nonproductive cycle for both parties. Consequently, the most successful approach to discipline is to provide each student with an education which adds value to his or her life.

The majority of discipline problems in most schools center on tardiness, unauthorized absences, disrupting classes and fighting. Each of these infractions can be addressed effectively by a program of discipline based on control theory. More serious infractions such as bringing a weapon to school, threatening another person or selling illegal substances must be addressed through district rules and the legal system. They cannot and should not be tolerated.

HELPING STUDENTS LEARN TO BE RESPONSIBLE

An effective discipline system is a teaching system. Its primary goal is to teach students better ways of behaving. Every student who acts out does so with the belief that it is the best thing she or he can do, given the circumstances in which he or she finds himself or herself. Teaching students to behave more responsibly is no different from teaching them anything else. In this context responsibility means that students are able to fulfill their needs without preventing others from fulfilling theirs. The high school is first and foremost a learning community, and each member of that community must be respected for what she or he needs to do to live a responsible life. When another student fails to respect that right, then she or he must be taught to stop the irresponsible behavior and start behaving more responsibly. Traditional practices of punishment only address the stop part of this two-part equation.

School Rules

The development of school rules should involve as many of the school participants as possible in their formulation. Begin by having discussions with small groups of students, teachers and staff focused on the questions, "What rules are necessary to get work done at our school? What rules do we need?" These discussions may take considerable time to conduct, but they are so important that the length of time it takes should not be viewed negatively. From these discussions, create a tentative list of school rules for discussion purposes only. Begin a second round of discussions with the same participants to see if there are suggestions for improving the tentative rules.

A second draft of the school rules should then be written and circulated to teachers for discussions with student groups. Feedback should be solicited. A third draft of the rules can then be written and circulated. This process is repeated until as many people as possible in the school community have had a chance to participate. Once a "final" list of rules is completed, they should be written, circulated to everyone in the school and signed. Signatures are important. They let everyone know that the rules are important; they have been read and agreed to by the school community.

A creative way for accomplishing this step involves placing the rules on a large sheet of butcher paper attached to a wall in a central location of the school. Students, teachers and staff would sign under the rules agreeing to live within their constraints for the good of the community. The list might say, "We the undersigned agree that the following rules are necessary for work to get done at our school. We further agree to uphold them in order that our school community can be a good place for all its members." The placement of the signed rules in a central location is important. It gives everyone a chance to see them on a daily basis.

In a school applying a constructivist approach, rules should never be written once and for all. They should be open to discussion and modified as appropriate. An orderly process should be established to permit rules to be challenged at any time. New students to the school should be taken to the rules mural during their orientation to the school and asked to sign them. Periodically, the principal should present the rules to the student body for deeper understanding.

Rules for Instructional Areas

In classroom settings and laboratories teachers should use the school rules as guidelines for developing additional rules necessary to get work done in a specific area. Again, it is best to involve the students when establishing the rules. These rules should be posted conspicuously in the instructional area and signed by the students and adults who come to the area to work. In addition to the rules it is also helpful for teachers to discuss procedures for meeting the rules. Procedures for entering and exiting an instructional area, collecting and returning papers, working cooperatively and asking for help are the minimum and should be developed and discussed often.

Positive Reinforcement

All school personnel must place a high value on positive behavior. They should look for students being responsible and let them know about it. Obviously, in some cases, it may require a longer stretch than in others. When each student has an adviser who remains with her or him for an extended period, it seems easier for positive actions to be acknowledged.

Enforcing the Rules

Each professional or staff member who has a continuing contact with a student should work to become a part of that student's quality world. When accomplished, it is much easier to say to a student who is breaking a school or an instructional area rule to please stop and get a positive response. Enforcing rules must be done consistently, and this is more easily achieved when professionals work together.

For many students, simply calling their irresponsible behavior to their attention and asking them to stop will correct the problem. For others, additional measures may be necessary. If students fail to respond favorably to several respectful requests to correct irresponsible behavior, then they should be asked to write a behavioral contract to resolve the problem.

A sample behavioral contract might include each of the following questions designed for students to think about the nature of the problem and what they can do about it.

(1) What were you doing when the problem started?

(2) Was it against the rules?

(3) Can you develop a plan so it doesn't happen again?

(4) What is that plan?

The first question gets the students to focus on their behavior. The second juxtaposes the behavior and the school/class/area rules. The third and fourth places the responsibility upon the student to develop an acceptable plan to correct the problem. It is always good practice to have students sign any behavioral contract that they develop. They are more apt to uphold a contract they develop and sign. Behavioral contracts are always signed by the teacher or staff member where the problem occurred. No teacher or staff member should sign a contract that (1) fails to address the problem appropriately or (2) is poorly written. Students must be taught that a behavioral contract is an important document.

Timeout

When a student refuses to develop a plan or when they repeatedly fail to fulfill a plan, it is necessary to escalate the process. The concept of "timeout" has been borrowed from athletics where a team often takes a timeout to rethink its strategy and to devise a better plan. In a school timeout can be in a classroom, an instructional space or in a room in the building separate from the instructional areas.

In an instructional area "timeout" can be a table or a carrel or an area physically separate from the rest of the students. While in timeout students are expected to write a behavioral contract to address their problem. There is no time limit nor is there any additional penalty.

Students may listen to discussions, presentations and whatever else is taking place. They may also work on instructional assignments during a timeout without a reduction in grade. Students are simply removed from interaction with other students until the problem is resolved with the person with whom they have the problem, usually the teacher.

Failure to resolve the problem in the instructional area timeout area causes a further escalation of the remedy. In this case students are sent to the schoolwide timeout room. Here their freedom is further restricted because there is no involvement in what is going on in the class or instructional area whatsoever. In the schoolwide timeout room students must complete a behavioral contract to address their problem. When completed, and at the convenience of the person with whom they have the problem, a conference is scheduled to review the provisions of the contract. If the person agrees that the student is serious and the plan is workable, he or she signs it and the student returns in good standing. If the plan is not acceptable, then the student goes back to the schoolwide timeout room to rethink and rewrite. The point to emphasize is that students are not reinstated automatically. They must be willing to address the problem in a mature manner. On the other hand, the teachers and staff must be reasonable in accepting plans and in helping students write them.

The schoolwide timeout room must be staffed by people who understand control theory. It is not a jail; it is a place where students go to think through a problem, to develop a different strategy and to change direction. The best people to staff timeout areas are counselors. After all, when a student is behaving inappropriately, who is better able to assist them to get back on track than a professional with counseling skills. If counselors are not available or willing, then a teacher or teachers may share the responsibility as part of their assignment. In some cases, a paraprofessional can staff timeout. It is important, however, that the person(s) in charge like students and fully understand control theory. Furthermore, teachers must understand that timeout should never be used as a threat. Threats and other coercive tactics interfere with the problem-solving environment.

Toleration Days

When students refuse to develop plans in the schoolwide timeout room, the next step is to send them home. They are instructed to work on the plan and to return to school when it is completed. Upon returning to school, they are interviewed by an administrator and returned to the schoolwide timeout room until a conference can be arranged with the teacher or staff person involved. Once again there is no direct re-entry. Students must do more than serve time; they must address their problem seriously. It is this component that differentiates toleration days from suspension. When a student is sent home, parents should be informed of the problem and what is expected of the student. Any school work completed while on a toleration day receives full credit. Some schools that use a control theory approach send students home for fighting on the first offense. They realize that it is impossible to resolve a problem when students are angry. Sending the students home for a day enables them to cool off so that the problem can be resolved when cooler heads prevail.

Serious Infractions

Behavior that threatens others or is in violation of school district rules or community laws must be handled differently. Moreover, there are some students who should probably be assigned to an alternative school within the district if one exists. Some students really need a change of venue in order to get a new start. Their view of their present school precludes any positive change. Students whose presence on the school campus pose a threat to students and adults must be removed. Fortunately, in most school settings these students are a small percentage of the total student body.

A PROBLEM-SOLVING ENVIRONMENT

Viewing student misbehavior as a problem to be solved is consistent with the philosophy undergirding a constructivist high school. All problems are individual in nature even though all humans are genetically bound to satisfy the same basic needs. How they choose to solve the problem is an individual decision. When students choose to act out and disrupt, they are doing so for reasons of their own. It is their interpretation of what is best for them at the moment. Discipline in a problem-solving context asks the students to think of other behaviors that will not infringe on other people's rights to satisfy their needs. This is not an easy lesson for most adolescents to learn. It takes time. There are no quick fixes to discipline problems. As Glasser affirms ". . . the only good solutions to discipline problems are systematic and long term" (1992, p. 140).

Two things can help with this process. The first involves teaching control theory to all students in the school. This can be accomplished through the social studies curriculum or homeroom or group guidance. It is important because if students know the theory behind the process they tend to do a better job of solving their own problems. Also knowing control theory can transfer to other areas of their lives. The second places trust upon the students to resolve their own problems. Insofar as possible, students should be asked to solve their own problems. Parents should be involved only sparingly. Often, when the school gets parents involved in a discipline problem, the student gets punished and then blames the school for causing the punishment she or he gets at home. "Calling in the parents is also an admission that the school cannot handle its own problems, an admission that managers should not make" (Glasser, 1992, p. 136).

Discipline problems are real problems. When schools say to students, "We believe you are capable of working out your own problems," trust between the student and the educators begins to take root. It is an opportunity to stress a philosophy and a set of skills which will empower students in the present and the future. In the long haul, the goal of effective schooling should be the elimination of any outward form of discipline system. Activities such as timeout are short-term measures to fill a vacuum while educators are refining their approach to schooling. When schools become caring places where students can learn to solve problems, there is less need for the defensive behavior which fosters antagonism between students and educators. In time, timeout rooms can be eliminated because there are no discipline problems serious enough to require them.

A good high school is a place where students work hard because they see what they are asked to do as valuable. They see teachers as friends who are there to help them solve problems. When students are disruptive, they are helped to see that their disruption is their problem and that receiving help in the solution of the problem is more important than administering punishment. As a high school moves toward a system of discipline that avoids coercion, several key elements should be considered. (1) A student's past behavior should not be invoked as part of a present problem. (2) All rules should be enforced calmly. (3) When

possible, it is helpful to ease tension with humor. (4) Solving behavioral problems requires a cooperative effort between educators and
students. (5) Long-term solutions to problems must be developed when
students are not angry or disruptive. (6) Educators must develop the
habit of reinforcing responsible behavior. (7) No matter how students
respond to the system, insist that they focus on what they can do to
prevent problems in the future. (8) Keep in mind that solving problems
is very often hard, but rewarding work.

First Steps

Step One

Invite administrators and respected teachers to read *Control Theory
in the Classroom* and discuss the contents. Create a list of study questions to guide the discussions. The book is short (137 pages) and
available in paperback. Each participant should have his or her personal copy. The study group should establish its own schedule and
meeting times. When the group has fully discussed the main ideas contained in the book and understands their implications for schooling, the
group should develop a plan for extending the discussions to other
members of the faculty. This might be done in a carefully planned
faculty meeting led by teachers and administrators from the group, by
having each member of the original discussion group invite one other
person on the faculty to form a second discussion group or by having
them accept responsibility for tutoring the others in the basic concepts
of control theory.

Step Two

Inquire into the effectiveness of school rules. Which ones seem to be
working for most of the faculty? Which ones are not? Perhaps a checklist could be created so that faculty could place a check beside the rules
that are working while leaving blank the space beside those which are
not. Report the results of the survey at a general faculty meeting.
Following the presentation of results, encourage cooperative groups of
faculty and administration to discuss any implications and make
specific recommendations. Ask for volunteers to conduct class meetings with students on rules.

Step Three

Create a sample format for conducting a class meeting with students. Distribute the format to the teacher volunteers and others who are interested. The sample questions might resemble the following:

(1) Definition: What are rules? Why do we have rules? Who makes rules? How are rules enforced? Are there some school rules that are better than others? Are there some school rules that should be changed? Are there some rules that cannot be changed?

(2) Personalize: Are there rules at home that you have to follow? Were you allowed to make any of the rules at home? In the classroom? Do you ever break rules? Talk about a time when you broke the rules.

(3) Challenge: Do you think a school could operate without rules? Why or why not? Can you think of some places where following rules is important? Can you think of any places where rules are not important? Suppose you were asked to create rules for the school. What would they be? Who should follow them? How should they be enforced?

Step Four

See the rules section of this chapter and follow as much of the procedure as you think possible.

Step Five

Ask for volunteers to teach control theory to students. Look at the course for middle level students called *Choice* written by Dr. William Glasser. See how much of this approach has application for your high school. The course comes with a workbook and videotape.

Step Six

See the process of enforcing rules outlined in this chapter. Use its content as the basis for reshaping how rules are enforced in your high school.

Note: Materials for helping faculty and students learn about control theory are available from Educator Training Center, 117 East 8th Street, Suite 810, Long Beach, CA 90813. Two videotapes which can help are "Control Theory: Successfully Educating Today's Students" (13 minutes) and "Control Theory in Schools: An Introduction" (42 minutes).

CHAPTER 9

Changing the Venues for Learning

Culture hides much more than it reveals and strangely enough what it hides, it hides most effectively from its own participants.—*Edward Hall*

THE LATE MARSHALL McLuhan quipped that he didn't know who discovered water, but he was certain it wasn't the fish. He elaborated by explaining that fish have no anti-environment which would enable them to perceive the element in which they live. Hence, they are affected by the water daily, but are not aware of the impact. He viewed this condition as analogous to the degree of awareness that people have to any environment created by new technology (McLuhan and Fiore, 1968). The new technology comes into people's lives and changes them without their conscious awareness. He used this thesis throughout several of his books to explain sudden changes in values, perceptions, and behaviors in individuals and groups of people.

Technology as an extension of the human body changes sense ratios so that the traditional classroom frequently conflicts with the tendencies that students bring to the school. The cooler medium of the printed word contradicts the hotter medium of the electronic environment in which the students live. They come to school "plugged in" to the events of the moment. When events happen in the world, they are known instantly whether it is the assassination of a world leader, the resignation of a president, riots in a major city, an airplane accident or the trial of a noted personality. They happen in our living rooms and the students are there. This is a much different scenario than the predominantly linear treatment of these events in a traditional classroom or textbook.

One only needs to spend some time at a place like Epcot Center in

Orlando, Florida, to gain an appreciation of the power of environment in learning. The dinosaur pavillion transports the participants back in time to experience a simulation of how things were at the time the dinosaurs roamed the planet. The "Living Seas" gives visitors the illusion that they are actually under the sea looking at the myriad life forms. A replication of the circulatory system of the human body places one inside so that he or she can experience the body from the inside out. All of these centers are representations of reality that engage the individual. They teach by their very existence.

Howard Gardner in *The Unschooled Mind: How Children Think and How Schools Should Teach* (1991) writes, "Much, if not most of what happens in schools happens because that is the way it was done in earlier generations, not because we have a convincing rationale for maintaining it today." He advocates schools in which the intuitive understandings of the students are both accepted and challenged by direct involvement in real-life experiences. In his judgment, these experiences can be provided by apprenticeships for each student in a multiage team with a community expert, by placement in a museum-type atmosphere in the community or by project learning in the school itself. According to Gardner, "Each of these settings has potential to engage contemporary students, to stimulate their understanding and, most importantly, to help them assume responsibility for their own future learning." By comparison he sees the present school settings as increasingly anachronistic to the development of understanding on the part of students (Gardner, 1991).

In a chapter from the monograph *Organizing for Learning: Toward the 21st Century,* Fenwick English (1989) predicts that the concept of the educational colony will replace the school as we know it. He describes the colony as a series of immersions where students learn about history and events by living them rather than studying about them. Building on the work of J. R. Anderson, English describes a series of learning environments in which students learn languages in the context of the culture in which it is indigenous. This is similar to the training Peace Corps volunteers receive to take their places in foreign lands. He asserts that most of the students could learn four to five different languages using this approach. In his school for 2088, total immersion replaces today's static separate-subject curriculum. Student placement into one of the living environments is based on a match between the student's knowledge, personal proclivities and learning orientations (English, 1989). Thus sophisticated technology is used to realize and extend the school environment into a personalized program geared to the learning needs and backgrounds of individual learners.

On a smaller scale, classrooms are learning environments created by teachers to help students master concepts and skills. The setting in which the learning is expected to take place influences the quality of the learning for each student. Students interact with the nature of that learning environment and derive different meanings dependent on their idiosyncratic characteristics. The kinds of environments that teachers create are powerful teachers which reinforce or counteract what is expected to be learned.

CHANGING THE SCHOOL ENVIRONMENT

When teachers understand the impact that the classroom itself can have on students and their learning, they can deliberately plan to construct them differently. Instead of the typical classroom with desks facing forward, the classroom can be redesigned with areas for independent pursuits, informal areas where students can work seated in comfortable furniture, areas for small group work and areas for teacher presentation. Moreover, the classroom can reflect the ongoing content with bulletin boards, walls and free-standing learning centers created to bring knowledge to life.

The idea of hidden curriculum is the one that is taught without most people being aware of it. Every school has a hidden curriculum. It is composed of the messages conveyed by policies, practices and norms. Educators praise students for timeliness, neatness and a host of other values. They describe good students in terms of respect toward the school, their teachers and the other students. Good students are expected to do their homework, sit up straight, speak when spoken to or raise their hands to speak. They aren't expected to question the content, the textbook or teacher. The hidden curriculum is a profound teacher. Like McLuhan's notion, "The media is the message," it may not be the only message, but it does teach silently.

Becoming aware of the importance of the silent teacher can lead us to take steps to understand the implications of our actions from a variety of perspectives. What we do may speak more loudly than our slogans and our rhetoric. Hence, if we are serious about creating a school environment for learning, then we must consider all the elements of the environment, the obvious and the not so obvious.

The setting in which students go to school teaches. Structuring that environment, therefore, should be done with care. I envision a school comprised of learning areas which reflect the content under study at all times. Quality student work should be on display from which other students can learn. Students should create learning materials for other students so as to apply and extend their own learning.

A SCHOOL FOR ALL REASONS

One such living and breathing example of a place where educators think seriously about the learning environment is the Thomas Haney Secondary Centre located in Maple Ridge, British Columbia. The school opened three years ago after very careful planning by the professional educators and the lay community. The design of the curriculum and the instructional program preceded the planning of the building and supports the work of the teachers and students. The school facilities are designed to support programs which encourage and promote individual student responsibility. There are no typical classroom spaces. Instead, there are individual and small group study areas, a building-wide computer network to allow for data access from terminals, resource areas from which students obtain some learning materials, quiet zones, zones for noisier activities, a great hall which offers unlimited opportunities for the displays of student work, offices for teachers and the flexibility to restructure space when appropriate. The science area gives the feeling of a real science laboratory where students work individually, in pairs or in teams on experiments contained in study guides or of their own selection. A business area integrates business curricula by simulating a business office in the community. Here, students get hands-on experiences. The curriculum affords students the opportunity to work in the community for extended periods. Physical education credit is awarded for coaching younger children, officiating in community leagues, ski trips, wilderness experiences, personal fitness and amateur competition. Such experiences bring the curriculum to life for many more students.

Learning guides, not textbooks, provide a variety of activities for each student. All students are expected to meet the Ministry of Education graduation requirements, but with flexibility. Different pathways for different students are policy, not novelty. When students cannot relate the pathways suggested by teachers, they are invited to create their own provided it meets the standards of quality control. Conventional courses are divided into four units with five learning guides developed for each unit. Students progress at their own rate and demonstrate their learning when they are ready to do so. Evaluation of student learning is based mostly on authentic kinds of assessment. Students have teacher advisers who work closely with them in building daily schedules, choosing courses and activities and monitoring academic progress.

The Thomas Haney School is a total environment for learning. All students have a part in constructing their own learning experiences. They choose activities and options that best reflect the way in which they learn. Direct assistance is provided students with evidence of weak cognitive skills. Lifelong learning is emphasized.

CONGENIAL ACRES OF JUNE

One option for any high school educator that can help create environments for learning is independent study. It was a regular part of the NASSP Model Schools Project in the late 1960s and early 1970s. Students were scheduled into large group, small group and independent study options for each of eight separate subjects. Independently, they worked on learning packages. In some cases, students were able to create their own independent study projects as an outgrowth of a learning package.

Independent study is not to be confused with unscheduled time when students may choose to do what they wish. (This was a popular option for students when modular schedules were in vogue.) Rather, it is a kind of study in which students work alone or with other students on projects of interest or on materials predetermined by the teacher. Probably the most effective independent pursuits are those that students construct for themselves. The projects can be part of classroom instruction or unrelated to classroom instruction. From the standpoint of effective learning environments, however, it is important that students see the connection between what is to be learned and improving their lives.

Czikszentmihalyi (1990) at the University of Chicago has written extensively about optimal experience in humans. He describes the motivation and hard work that individuals display in achieving such high level accomplishments as mountain climbing and marathon running. These accomplishments all stem from the internal motivation to achieve. He describes the true learning experience in school as one that emanates from an individual's desire to extend his or her knowledge and skills. It is intrinsic to the task and idiosyncratic to the individual learner. He envisions schools where students are "happily concentrated" at tasks which they help create.

One only has to think of the instrinsic involvement of the science student getting ready for the district fair, or the band preparing for district competition or the athletic team devoting more hours to practice than the individual members do to academic study. All are willing to endure a plethora of hardships to improve their skills. These "congenial acres of June," as I call them, are the stuff from which quality is made.

High school programs which include an opportunity for independent study outside of the classroom setting can work, but they require organization. Even though the adolescent of today is more sophisticated than his counterpart of twenty years ago, organizing one's time for serious study is still a learned ability. It requires guidance. Appointing a staff member to give leadership to the schoolwide independent study is important. It should be a person who understands the difficulties of doing independent investigations as well as a person knowledgeable about the inquiry process itself. Students should be scheduled with this person for weekly seminars and regular conferences.

The "coordinator of independent study," as I shall call this person, should help each student to identify and define a project for investigation. As a generalist this person takes responsibility for defining the parameters of the program and working with the students. He or she also helps the students to locate a mentor or a learning preceptor who is proficient in the area of investigation. The threesome then becomes a team working toward the completion of the project.

One successful procedure is to design a contract for each student completing an independent study project. The contract includes objectives, activities, a schedule and a means of evaluation. It should be signed by the student, the coordinator of independent study and the learning preceptor. A copy is given to all three parties. The coordinator monitors the student's completion of the contract during regularly scheduled conferences. At the completion of the project, the student should present his or her findings to the faculty, the community or to interested students.

Figure 9.1 shows a sample format for a student-developed contract that can be applied to a variety of learning areas.

It is important that the student have an opportunity to report what he or she has discovered. This report can be completed in written form, as well as oral, and should enhance the academic nature of the school community. Written reports can be added to the library database and made available to other students. Expositions of student work can be scheduled at different times during the year. The expositions should offer a platform for students to present their projects to others.

COMMUNITY LEARNING CENTERS

Community-based learning is not a new idea. It has been a part of many high school programs for several decades. Only in the past few years, however, has this type of experiential education gained in popularity. It can be an elective in the social studies curriculum or a graduation requirement for all students monitored by the homeroom teacher or teacher adviser. In either case students complete hours of voluntary service in elementary schools, day care centers, nursing homes, centers for students with special needs, hospitals, centers providing meals for the homeless or within their high schools as peer counselors and tutors. In some instances, for example, the North Carolina School for Mathematics and Science, the students must work each semester in the school offices, the school cafeteria or the school grounds.

The "Executive Internship" is a national program that offers energetic students an opportunity to explore a career of interest for several hours per week for a semester or a full year. Internships provide an inside look at an occupation or a career; they stretch the written word to include the demands of a position, the organizational structure to which one must relate, the expectations for employees and the decision-making process in the actual world. Students learn first hand about law, medicine, communications, journalism, government, social services, business, banking and the arts.

Community study encourages students to participate actively in community problems. Usually as an outgrowth of a class, students get involved in the solutions to problems and needs of their own community. Conducting surveys or ecological studies, attending meetings of the city council, checking on traffic patterns at busy intersections, investigating community feelings about annexation plans—all instill a

Sample Student Contract

Directions: This contract should be completed in full by the requesting student. It is the student's responsibility to obtain the signatures of his/her teacher, adviser, learning preceptor and parent(s). All persons must approve the contract prior to its implementation. A copy of the completed contract must be presented to all persons who have signed the agreement. Responsibility for monitoring progress in completing the contract rests with the student and the teacher.

Subject(s): _____

Title of Project: _____

_____

Objective(s): _____

_____

_____

Resources: Provide a list of resources you will use in completing the project. Include people, places, and materials.

Time Budget: List the activities you will undertake in completing the contract and estimate the time each will take. Project a completion date and a date when you will be ready to present your findings to faculty and peers.

Evaluation: Final evaluation will be determined cooperatively by the teacher, the student and the learning preceptor and will be based on the quality of the final project and the public presentation. It is expected that all work will be of high quality.

Signatures: _____ (Student) _____ (Date)

_____ (Teacher) _____ (Date)

_____ (Preceptor) _____ (Date)

_____ (Parent) _____ (Date)

Figure 9.1. A Sample Student Contract. (If a school has a person who directs independent study, then he or she should coordinate all contract learning and sign the contract also.)

reality to school subjects and a chance to apply what is learned in the classroom to issues of substance in the community.

Much like independent study, students who do volunteer work or complete internships or who apply their classroom learning to community problems need venues where they can reflect on their experiences. Weekly seminars led by teachers can often provide such opportunities.

OPEN-ENDED CLASSROOM MEETINGS

In his book *Schools without Failure* (1969), Dr. William Glasser introduced the concept of classroom meetings. The classroom meeting involves an entire class of thirty or more students and teacher assembled for the purpose of talking about a subject of importance to the group. Of the three types of classroom meetings, the open-ended one seems best related to the idea of students constructing their own meanings from the content.

Students and teacher sit in a circle so that they can see and hear each other clearly. Names are important. Each student wears a name tag or writes his name on a piece of paper or tag board placed at his feet. The idea is that all students refer to students by name. After awhile, this procedure is not necessary. The teacher, as leader, is always nonjudgmental. He or she never comments on the rightness or wrongness of a response. Among the purposes of the open-ended classroom meeting are: (1) to have all students participate in the discussion, (2) to explore various perspectives on topics of importance, (3) to provide opportunities for insightful, critical and divergent thinking and (4) to furnish a channel for relevancy through discussion of subjects important to students.

Topics can be selected by students or by the teacher. As a beginning, the teacher can introduce the idea by selecting a topic which he or she believes meets two criteria: relevant and thoughtful. These two criteria should always be foremost when selecting topics. Several topics which might fit the criteria are: AIDS, intelligence, selecting a college, affirmative action policies, gender bias, censorship, crime and capital punishment. The teacher then prepares a list of stimulating, thought-provoking and challenging questions to guide the discussion.

Three levels of questions are constructed as follows:

(*1*) Level I—Define the topic. Ask the students for their definition,

"What does it mean to be gender-biased?" You want to focus on the definitions the students offer. Search for different points of view. Build subsequent questions on student answers.

(2) Level II — Personalize the topic. Relate the topic to the students' worlds. Ask questions about the student, his family, his friends, etc. For example, "Can you describe an instance in your life when you received unfair treatment because you were a female? a male?" "Are there things you feel you are not allowed to do because you are female? male?" "Can you recall any stories you were told or you read as you were growing up that taught gender bias?"

(3) Level III — Challenge, extension. Encourage diverse ideas by asking questions for which there can be several answers. Ask questions which search for what, what if, could we, should we. Guide discussion to encourage the extension of ideas. For example, "How do you think we can eliminate gender bias completely?" "What do you think our society might be like if we did?" "What would it be like if we didn't?" "Are there jobs that males should do that females shouldn't?" "Should females be assigned combat duty in the military?" "Why or why not?"

An example of a plan for conducting a classroom meeting on the topic of violence is presented in Figure 9.2.

Conducting classroom discussions is a skill which all teachers can learn. It takes practice, however. Mastery can take as many as 100 discussions, but positive results can be attained in the first session. Classroom meetings can be conducted during homerooms, or during class time or during scheduled times during the week. One classroom meeting per week is reasonable. It is time well-spent. Students practice thinking behavior and they learn to see the world from a variety of perspectives. The classroom meetings, moreover, challenge the concepts that students have learned and help them to integrate new knowledge into existing categories of knowledge. (For information about classroom meetings: write to Educator Training Center, 117 East Eighth Street, Suite 810, Long Beach, California 90813.)

THE SOCRATIC SEMINAR

Socratic seminars are a part of the *Paideia Proposals,* as described by Mortimer Adler (1982). It is one of the most innovative dimensions

Violence
Suggested Questions

Define:	1.	What is violence?
	2.	Give some examples of violent behavior.
	3.	Give some examples of how violence is presented in television shows, movies.
	4.	Are violent acts always overt? Can they be subtle?
Personalize:	1.	Describe a television show which you recently watched which contained violence.
	2.	Describe a movie which you recently saw which contained violence.
	3.	How did the television show or movie affect your behavior?
	4.	Describe any school episodes which you considered violent.
	5.	How do school rules curtail student violence?
	6.	Describe an episode in your life which you regard as violent.
Challenge:	1.	If you were the owner of a major television network, would you eliminate violence?
	2.	Same question for owner of a movie studio.
	3.	Do you think that exposure to violent programming or movies over an extended period of time affects people's behavior negatively? Why or why not?
	4.	Is violence something that will always be with us?
	5.	How might violence be eliminated in our society? our city? our school?
	6.	What is the effect of laws on reducing violent acts?
	7.	Suppose you wanted to reduce violence in our community. How would you start?

Figure 9.2. Sample Plan for an Open-Ended Classroom Meeting. (Questions may be added as discussion dictates.)

of these proposals. The method of the Socratic seminar is one of inquiry and challenging questions. The seminars are conducted in seminar rooms or their equivalent by teacher leaders. Groups of approximately fifteen students are recommended. The teacher sits at the table with the students as an equal, although a little older and wiser. Seminars are usually scheduled once per week for ninety minutes.

Seminar topics serve as inquiries into important ideas. The point is to get students to engage great ideas and to discuss them with their peers. The teacher guides the discussion asking penetrating questions throughout the discussion. Students have their minds addressed in a challenging way. They are asked to express their thoughts and to defend their opinions in a rational form.

William Bennett's, *The Book of Virtues* (1993) is an excellent source for ideas and reading materials for the seminars. The book is divided into ten chapters, each focused on a specific quality—self-discipline, compassion, responsibility, friendship, work, courage, perseverance, honesty, loyalty and faith. Although Bennett describes the book as a "how to book for moral literacy," it appears much more than that. Used for Socratic seminars, the documents, stories and poems can serve as springboards for intellectual inquiry on the important ideas of our culture.

Under the quality of courage, students could read *Rosa Parks* by Kai Friese and Patrick Henry's speech on *Liberty or Death*. For responsibility, they could read *The Declaration of Independence,* or Martin Luther King's *Letter from a Birmingham Jail*. The genius of Bennett's collection is that they are short pieces that can be read in reasonable time, perfect for the notion of the Socratic seminar.

Plans for Socratic seminars are best developed by groups of teachers (see Figure 9.3 for an example). In a given school year of nine months, each month might focus on a different idea. A group of teachers could volunteer to develop plans for the four monthly seminars for a given idea. The plans would include reading selections, sample questions, staff development and providing sufficient copies for students. In order to achieve the seminar group size, all professionals in the high school would participate, including the principal.

Taking time each week to discuss important concepts and ideas builds an academic climate in the school. Students and teachers take time to become familiar with the documents and literature which have made our country great and to share interpretations and opinions.

THE ENVIRONMENT AS TEACHER

The students who attend our high schools are much more in touch with the simultaneity of events than were the students of twenty years ago. Today's technological revolution has created a marketing-information age where the future belongs to those persons who can acquire, store and apply knowledge creatively. It also belongs to those persons who can solve problems and generate new knowledge. As the

---

Lincoln's Gettysburg Address

1. What were the circumstances surrounding President Lincoln giving this famous address?
2. Why do you think he chose to give the address in Gettysburg, Pennsylvania?
3. What was President Lincoln's message to the citizens of the United States? to the world?
4. What was the cause for which so many gave "a full measure of devotion?"
5. In your opinion was it a just cause?
6. Are there similar causes today for which men and women might give a full measure of devotion?
7. What does "government of the people, by the people, for the people" mean to you?
8. How does the content of the Gettysburg address impact our lives today?
9. Are conflicts over principle inevitable? How are they best resolved?
10. Why do you think historians rate Lincoln's Gettysburg Address as the greatest speech ever given on American soil?

Figure 9.3. Sample Questions for Conducting a Socratic Seminar on the Gettysburg Address.

world becomes more complex, new ways of seeing are necessary for survival.

The technological environment like all environments shapes all of us. High school students come plugged into the sights and sounds of the universe. They channel surf across satellites to catch passing glimpses of events, persons, MTV, sit coms, quiz shows and cartoons. A school environment that does not acknowledge this phenomenon is out of touch with the new contingencies and makes connections for students more difficult to attain.

Many of us have lauded student teaching as the most valuable experience in our preservice education for becoming a teacher. In so doing, we were reinforcing the role of immersion in the learning process. All classrooms, no matter how they are fashioned, teach, and like McLuhan's comment about the fish, we educators may be the last people to discover the impact.

First Steps

Step One

Take color slide photographs that illustrate the hidden curriculum.

Pictures might include classroom arrangements, school rules, size of offices, grouping practices, advertisements posted on school walls, the library-media center use and so on. At a faculty meeting or, even better, at smaller discussion group meetings show the slides and ask teachers to comment on what they convey. For example, how do our grouping practices support the notion of equal opportunity and social mobility? or how does our school reward structure encourage students to do work for the joy of doing it?

Step Two

Ask for volunteers to visit a local museum and report back to the faculty on what they discovered about environments and student learning. Ask two or three students who work in the community to share with the faculty what they have learned and are learning from the placement.

Step Three

Ask for volunteers to serve on a task force to investigate ways to restructure the school purposely to teach certain values to students. Perhaps a theme or a series of themes could focus the school's attention for a specified time. Themes such as, "Who Am I? What Is My Family?" could cut across subject matter lines and unify seemingly disparate content.

Step Four

Offer a staff development workshop on open-ended classroom meetings. Arrange for continuing education points or course credit for the participants. Use material from the Educator Training Center in California or have an experienced teacher or consultant lead the workshop. If possible, have the principal and a teacher share the leadership responsibility. Demonstrate a classroom meeting with real students as the teachers observe. When completed, dismiss the students and ask for questions from the observing teachers. Brainstorm ideas for classroom meetings and have the workshop participants work in pairs to create suitable questions following the prescribed format. After revising the questions based on review by the workshop participants, each teacher should attempt to conduct a class meeting and report back to the group in two weeks. This procedure continues for the remainder of the workshop.

Step Five

Upon completion of the workshop have the teachers identify teachers who did not choose to attend the initial workshop and talk with them about what was learned, its benefits and shortcomings. Invite others to participate in a follow-up staff development workshop.

Step Six

Identify a cadre of teachers who could begin work on transforming their classrooms or instructional areas into venues for learning. The point of all this is to teach by example and to work out from the "soft centers" of the faculty to others less initially inclined. When examples are established, they can serve as teaching components based on the Chinese proverb, "I hear and I forget, I see and I remember, I do and I understand."

PART FIVE

SUMMARY

CHAPTER 10

In Perspective

The woods are lovely, dark, and deep. But I have promises to keep, And miles to go before I sleep, And miles to go before I sleep.—*Robert Frost*

CONSTRUCTIVISM IS NOT some esoteric theory for round-table discussions by scholars nor is it a fad that will ascend briefly and then disappear. Rather, it is a different view of teaching and learning that has been germinating for several decades. Historians can trace many constructivist ideas to the writings of John Dewey early in this century and later to the work of Piaget. Constructivist thinking is grounded in solid research in the behavioral sciences. It differs from traditional stimulus-response psychology in several important ways. To the constructivist:

(1) Learning is an active process. Learners apply knowledge and skills to the solutions of meaningful problems.

(2) Learning is developmental and proceeds along a continuum from naive interpretations of concepts to more sophisticated ones. As learners mature intellectually, they are able to grasp ideas more analytically. They also see the bigger picture.

(3) Learning is internally driven. The meaning assigned to external reality is resident in the individual's cognitive structure. All learners are really internally motivated. External motivation is more fiction than fact.

(4) Learning is more meaningful when it occurs in context. The closer the school learning tasks match the situations in which the information and skills will be used, the more likely learners will see the value of what they are asked to do.

(5) Learning is facilitated by interactions with others. Learners refine and expand their understanding of concepts by working closely with individuals who are functioning at different levels of development.

(6) Learning is substantially influenced by the learner's level of intellectual development. Optimal learning tasks are those that are within the scope of the learner's development, yet challenging enough to cause him or her to stretch intellectually.

(7) Learning is more than what is measured by objective paper and pencil tests.

(8) Learning is best when it is self-referencing. Continuous improvement, what the Japanese label *kaizen,* results from learners thinking about the nature of their own learning process.

(9) Learning involves four components: acting, thinking, feeling and physiology. Only acting and thinking can be controlled by learners. Feeling and physiology accompany changes in acting and thinking. What a learner chooses to do affects all four components.

The key elements of constructivism provide a framework for making high schools more responsive to the needs of individual students. An intensive focus on individual students and their development is the theme that distinguishes a restructured high school from a traditional one. Group-paced instruction, objective testing and rewards and punishments, once deemed venerable ways to get students to buckle down and work hard, appear no longer viable. Since the 1950s a progression of research findings and theory support the common wisdom that people are different. A high school where individual differences are systematically diagnosed and accommodated through variegated instruction is one that increases hope for all learners, and hope is the beginning of opportunity.

CONSTRUCTIVIST IMPLICATIONS FOR HIGH SCHOOLS IN REVIEW

Curriculum

National efforts by professional associations to identify standards and benchmarks in subject areas hold promise for individual high schools.

Combining these standards with state-adopted curriculum frameworks can provide guidelines for establishing essential outcomes for all students. In light of how the national standards have been written, this is no easy undertaking. Once established, teachers are then responsible for helping students see the connection between essential outcomes and likely success in life. Schools associated with the *Paideia Proposals* share the common belief that "the best education for the best students is the best education for all students." The belief seems an appropriate rallying cry as high school educators contemplate changes. Dumbing down the curriculum for students judged slower seems out of step in a world where international events shape national, state and local policies and where events are televised into millions of homes almost at the moment they happen.

Higher standards for all students are possible, but they must be achieved one student at a time. In this regard, personalizing the educational process means diagnosis, prescription, implementation and evaluation. It implies a cycle of professional activity which begins by gathering salient data about an individual student's learning history, learning style and developmental characteristics. This database is used to develop a personalized educational plan for each student in the high school. The plan then becomes a basis for adapting instruction to individual differences. The last step, evaluation, looks at student learning as a measure of the success of instruction. The cycle then begins anew.

Cognitive-Learning Style

As a term, *learning style* is frequently referenced in the professional literature about teaching and learning. In plain language it refers to how students learn and how they like to learn. The "how students learn" refers to the cognitive elements of style and the "how they like to learn" refers to the preferences that students have for different parts of the learning environment. The *Learning Style Profile (LSP)*, a second generation learning style instrument, assesses twenty-four elements of learning style. Administering the *LSP* to students upon entering high school provides teachers with salient information from which to develop appropriate instructional strategies. Research shows that matching instruction to individual student learning styles results in higher academic achievement, reduces discipline referrals and improves attitudes toward schooling in general. When students are taught about their learning styles, they are able to make adjustments in their home and school environments to increase the likelihood that they will comprehend new and difficult material.

The Thinking Imperative

The SCANS Report [The Secretary's Commission for Achieving Necessary Skills (1991)] identifies thinking skills as one of the three foundations supporting the competencies workers will need to take their place in "work forces dedicated to excellence." The report further describes thinking as making decisions, thinking creatively, solving problems, visualizing solutions and knowing how to learn (p. xviii). Conceptualizing thinking skills on a continuum with cognitive skills (controls) at one end and reflective thinking at the other provides a framework for developing higher-order thinking for all students. Students with weaknesses in specific cognitive skills will benefit from intensive instruction to augment the specific skills. Students with relative strengths in cognitive skills can advance along the continuum by applying the skills to generic or subject-specific settings. A new faculty position, cognitive resource teacher, seems a logical addition to a high school faculty dedicated to helping all students become effective learners.

Teaching thinking across all areas of the curriculum gives students opportunities to practice in a variety of settings. Including problem-solving activities in all areas of the curriculum gives students opportunities to apply knowledge in real-life settings. Working cooperatively in problem-solving teams gives students the opportunity to learn from each other. Placing teachers and other adults on the teams enhances the possibilities of all learners on the team.

Organizing for Learning

Procrustes was the man in Greek mythology who had one bed for overnight guests. If the guest was too short, he stretched him to fit the bed. If the guest was too long, he removed parts of his body until he fit the bed. In many respects the practices of ability grouping and age-related grouping appear similar to Procrustean thinking. There is ample research which shows the deleterious effects of ability grouping. Yet ability grouping is found in most, if not all, high schools. The idea of inclusion makes good sense for more than students labeled as exceptional.

There appears to be a rebirth of interest in the nongraded, ungraded or multiaged high school as a way to accommodate individual student differences and to raise the quality of student work overall. The graded school was an import from Prussia during the nineteenth century. Horace Mann was impressed with the graded schools in Prussia and upon his return to the United States he urged the adoption of a similar system. The first graded school is traced to the Quincy Grammar School in Quincy, Massachusetts, established circa 1848. By 1870, the system of graded schools was a fixture in all school districts.

The graded school was a monument to the administrative need to classify large numbers of students entering the public schools during the latter half of the nineteenth century. Efficiency, however, was gained at the expense of regimentation which has remained with the schools for over a century. Ostensibly, the time is right to call into question the practice of grouping by age and grouping by ability.

Professionalizing Teaching

Teaching must be transformed from a solitary activity to a collaborative one. The practice of isolating teachers and students in self-contained classrooms for 180–185 days annually fails to serve either teachers or students adequately. Teachers need time to prepare materials, to work individually with students, to improve their skills, to develop presentations and to assess their progress. These professional activities are impossible to achieve when teachers are faced with five classes and approximately 150 students per day. Teaming with other teachers can provide a degree of flexibility to allow for some of these important activities to take place on "company time."

Teachers are viewed as lead managers. They model rather than tell students what to do; they engage students in discussions of quality work; they help students to evaluate their own products; they create learning environments free of fear and coercion; they send invitations to students to learn.

The addition of paraprofessionals and student teachers to teaching teams provides additional flexibility to the teaching staff. Many of the tasks that teachers are currently assigned can be done easily by others with less formal training. Bus duty, hall duty, cafeteria duty and other general supervisory activities must be done but do not require a bachelor's or master's degree. Trade-offs enable teachers to devote important time to action research projects, advising students or developing units for instruction. Teaching is easy when students are highly motivated to do the work. It is difficult when they are not. Most public school students are in school because they have to be. The real measure of a teaching professional is the ability to get students to do some quality work and to internalize habits of mind which ensure quality performance wherever they go following graduation.

Scheduling

Contextual learning and problem solving require extended periods of time. The traditional schedule with forty-five to fifty-five minute periods each day does not facilitate the completion of in-depth learning tasks. The Carnegie unit, an artifact of an era when time and motion studies reigned supreme, provides only an indirect measure of student achievement. Redefining graduation requirements in terms of outcomes and exhibitions focuses directly on learning and shifts the emphasis from time to performance.

The current popularity of block scheduling is a tacit admission that traditional schedules do not adequately support student learning. The various forms of block schedules are a transition from the rigidities of the old scheduling model to the flexibility of a personalized model. A personalized schedule matches time with the activities to be accomplished and places control in the purview of teachers and students.

Managing Students

Every human being is internally motivated to satisfy basic needs. From birth the human organism experiences pleasure when needs are satisfied and pain when they are not, high school students included. They are internally motivated to satisfy their needs for survival, belonging, power, freedom and fun. When the needs are satisfied in the high school setting, students are less likely to act out and cause problems. When the needs are not satisfied in the high school setting, the students irritate educators who in turn irritate them.

Helping students behave responsibly means helping them to satisfy their needs without infringing on the ability of other students and adults to satisfy theirs. When all works well, a win-win situation exists. Unfortunately, the high school is not a perfect world and acts of student irresponsibility occur. How educators choose to deal with these acts makes an important difference. If interventions are timely, consistent and sensitive to the perceptions of the offended and the offender, then positive learning is possible. Irresponsible acts on the part of students must be stopped and a new responsible behavior learned. Discipline involves teaching. When high schools resort to punishment of students for rule infractions, it tells the student to stop what they are doing, but it does not teach them a better way. Punishment has no teaching component. In a high school restructured from a constructivist point of view irresponsible behaviors are seen as opportunities to resolve problems in a thoughtful manner.

Creating Venues

All school settings are venues for learning. The school environment by its existence shapes its inhabitants. Hidden curricula abound in every high school. The reflective educator understands this phenomenon and works to make all hidden curricula overt. Classrooms and teaching spaces should reflect the content under study. Quality works and quality works-in-progress should be exhibited in all areas of the school for students to study and emulate. Student contracts can tailor the curriculum to individual student interests. Community placements offer an array of opportunities for student growth from problem solving to content learning. Cognitive apprenticeships place students in close proximity with preceptors, mentors and other experts so that students can expand their problem-solving repertoires.

The location of learning should match the purposes of the specific learning task. Questions, such as where is the best place for this learning to be accomplished and with whom, should guide decisions as to where students should be scheduled for optimal learning. In some instances working at home with a computer and modem is the best setting. In other instances spending extended time in a laboratory, hospital, office or even another city, state or country is the best setting. The outlines which appear to separate the school buildings from the rest of the community are then gradually eroding. Where one ends and the other begins will soon be difficult to discern.

WHERE TO START

Every high school seems to have its own nature. It is a combination of the idiosyncracies of faculty, staff, parents and community. Even the degree of support for change varies from school district to school district. Consequently, this book advances no engineer's model of how a high school should look. Much like people, schools are learning organizations reflecting the stages of development individuals go through as they learn to structure and restructure knowledge at higher levels. It would be presumptuous to suggest a universal model applicable to all high schools.

One overriding assumption does appear evident. The goal of helping all students succeed in school requires that *all* high schools make some kind of change. It is the premise of this book that the changes should reflect a constructivist perspective. For many students the high school experience represents their last chance to learn to be effective learners. If they fail to master essential skills for learning while students, they face an uncertain future in a world where information is the chief currency. While world-class educational standards may be difficult to pin down, they are approximated when *all* students succeed at challenging learning tasks.

Forecasting the future is at best tenuous work. It is always limited by present circumstances and present perceptions. Despite these limitations there are competencies which appear necessary for citizens to deal more effectively with the present and the future when it becomes the present. These competencies include: making sense of information expanding at exponential rates, identifying and solving complex problems, creating new knowledge from existing knowledge, respecting others and working cooperatively with them, conserving and expanding democratic values and finding work which coincides with one's talents and strengths.

Secretary of Labor Robert Reich indicates that investment in two stable resources will ensure our nation's future — people and infrastructure. Of the two, high schools are institutions with high-stakes investments in people. In examining the growing prison population, one is struck by several facts. Most prisoners come from lower socioeconomic backgrounds, tend to be minority, are barely literate and are high school dropouts. Yet each of them was at one time a student in a high school in this country who had needs, interests and dreams that for various reasons were not fulfilled. Whether they would have fared better in a school structured by a constructivist approach is speculation.

The rhetoric of politicians and business leaders encourages educators to develop "break the mold" schools. Research provides support for new ways of learning. The choices that we make can increase the chances for *all* students to learn effectively, or they can maintain a precarious status quo. Many educators enjoy talking about change as long as it doesn't involve changing what they do. Unfortunately, time is running short. Initiating a journey toward constructivism means that the familiar characteristics of the high school will change, causing the professionals who inhabit the schools to change. But change is clearly the only stability that will endure. The present is merely prologue.

Adler, M. 1982. *The Paideia Proposals: An Educational Manifesto.* New York: Macmillan.

Anderson, R. H. and B. N. Pavan. 1993. *Nongradedness: Helping It to Happen.* Lancaster, PA: Technomic Publishing Co., Inc.

Bauersfeld, H. "Classroom Cultures from a Social Constructivist Perspective," *Educational Studies in Mathematics,* 23(5):467–481.

Bennett, W. J. 1993. *The Book of Virtues.* New York: Simon & Schuster.

Berliner, D. C. 1992. *Educational Reform in an Era of Disinformation.* Paper presented in the meetings of the American Association of Colleges for Teacher Education, San Antonio, Texas.

Betts, F. 1994. *What's All the Noise About? Constructivism in the Classroom.* Unpublished paper.

Brooks, J. G. and Brooks, M. G. 1993. *The Case for Constructivist Classrooms.* Alexandria, VA: Association for Supervision and Curriculum Development.

Brown, B. F. 1963. *The Nongraded High School.* Englewood Cliffs, NJ: Prentice-Hall.

Buffie, E. G. and J. M. Jenkins. 1971. *Curriculum Development in Nongraded Schools.* Bloomington, IN: Indiana University Press.

Business Week. 1992. "Can the Private Sector Save Our Schools?" September 14, 1992: 70–85.

Carroll, J. M. 1994. "The Copernican Plan Evaluated: The Evolution of a Revolution," *Phi Delta Kappan,* 76(2):105–113.

Carson, C. C., R. M. Huelskamp and T. D. Woodall. 1991. *Perspectives on Education in America.* Albuquerque, NM: Sandia National Laboratories.

Clark, W. A. 1994. "Partnerships in Pennsylvania," *The High School Magazine,* 2(2):22–24.

Clerk, F. E. 1928. *A Description and Outline of the Operation of the Adviser-Personnel Plan at New Trier High School.* Winnetka, IL.

151

Coloroso, B. 1994. *Kids Are Worth It! Giving Your Child the Gift of Inner Discipline.* New York: William Morrow and Company, Inc.

Corey, S. M. 1953. *Action Research to Improve School Practices.* New York: Teachers College, Columbia University.

Czikszentmihalyi, M. 1990. *Flow: The Psychology of Optimal Experience.* New York: Harper & Row, Inc.

Deming, W. E. 1986. *Out of the Crisis.* Cambridge: Massachusetts Institute of Technology Center for Advanced Engineering Study.

Edwards, J. 1991. "To Teach Responsibility, Bring Back the Dalton Plan," *Phi Delta Kappan.* 73(1):398–401.

English, F. W. 1989. "A School for 2088," in *Organizing for Learning: Toward the 21st Century,* H. J. Walberg and J. J. Lane, eds., Reston, VA: National Association of Secondary School Principals, pp. 89–97.

English, F. W. 1992. *Deciding What to Teach and Test.* Newbury Park, CA: Corwin Press.

English, F. W. 1993. "Changing the Cosmology of the School Schedule," in *Timepiece: Extending and Enhancing Learning Time,* L. Anderson and H. J. Walberg, eds., Reston, VA: National Association of Secondary School Principals, pp. 23–29.

Feldman, D. 1980. *Beyond Universals in Cognitive Development.* Ablex Publishing Corporation.

Friedland, S. 1994. "The Essential Elements for Success," *The High School Magazine. Norwood, NJ,* 1(3):29–33.

Gardner, H. 1991. *The Unschooled Mind: How Children Think and How Schools Should Teach.* New York: Basic Books.

Glasser, W. 1969. *Schools without Failure.* New York: Harper & Row, Inc.

Glasser, W. 1972. *The Identity Society.* New York: Harper & Row Publishers.

Glasser, W. 1981. *Stations of the Mind.* New York: Harper & Row Publishers.

Glasser, W. 1986. *Control Theory in the Classroom.* New York: Harper & Row Publishers.

Glasser, W. 1992. *The Quality School: Managing Students without Coercion.* New York: Harper Perennial.

Glatthorn, A. 1994. "Constructivism: Implications for Curriculum," *International Journal of Educational Reform,* 3(4):449–455.

Goodlad, J. I. and R. H. Anderson. 1963. *The Nongraded Elementary School.* New York: Harcourt, Brace & World.

Griggs, S. A. 1991. *Learning Styles Counseling.* Ann Arbor, MI: ERIC Counseling and Personnel Services Clearinghouse.

Havighurst, R. J. 1948. *Development Tastes and Education.* New York: David Mckay Company, Inc.

Herrnstein, R. J. and C. Murray. 1994. *The Bell Curve: Intelligence and Class Structure in American Life.* New York: The Free Press.

Hodgkinson, H. L. 1985. *All One System: Demographics of Education – Kindergarten through Graduate School.* Washington, DC: Institute for Educational Leadership, Inc.

Hottenstein, D. and C. Malatesta. 1993. "Putting a School in Gear with Intensive Scheduling," *The High School Magazine,* 1(2):28–29.

Howard, E. R. and J. W. Keefe. 1993. *Suggested Components for a School Design Statement.* Reston, VA: National Association of Secondary School Principals.

Jacobs, H. H. 1989. "Design Options for an Integrated Curriculum," in *Interdisciplinary Curriculum: Design and Implementation,* H. H. Jacobs, ed., Alexandria, VA: Association for Supervision and Curriculum Development, pp. 13–24.

Jenkins, J. M. 1992. *Advisement Programs: A New Look at an Old Practice.* Reston, VA: National Association of Secondary School Principals.

Jenkins, J. M., C. A. Letteri and P. Roselund. 1990. *Developing Cognitive Skills.* Reston, VA: National Association of Secondary School Principals.

Johnson, W. B. and A. H. Packer. 1987. *Workforce 2000.* Indianapolis, IN: Hudson Institute.

Jonassen, D. H. 1991. "Objectives vs. Constructivism: Do We Need a New Philosophical Design," *Educational Technology Research and Development,* 39(3):3–5, 14.

Kamii, C., F. B. Clark and A. Dominick. 1994. "The Six National Goals: A Road to Disappointment," *Phi Delta Kappan,* 75(9):672–677.

Keefe, J. W. 1987. "Development of the NASSP Learning Style Profile," in *Profiling and Utilizing Learning Style,* J. W. Keefe, ed., Reston, VA: National Association of Secondary School Principals.

Keefe, J. W. 1989. *Accommodating Perceptual Study and Instructional Preferences.* Reston, VA: National Association of Secondary School Principals.

Keefe, J. W. 1989. "Personalized Education," in *Organizing for Learning: Toward the 21st Century,* H. J. Walberg and J. J. Lane, eds., Reston, VA: National Association of Secondary School Principals, pp. 72–81.

Keefe, J. W. 1992. "Thinking about the Thinking Movement," in *Teaching for Thinking,* J. W. Keefe and H. J. Walberg, eds., Reston, VA: National Association of Secondary School Principals.

Keefe, J. W. and J. M. Jenkins, eds. 1991. *Instructional Leadership Handbook, 2nd ed.,* Reston, VA: National Association of Secondary School Principals.

Keefe, J. W. and J. S. Monk. 1986. *Learning Style Profile Examiner's Manual.* Reston, VA: National Association of Secondary School Principals.

Kendall, J. S. and R. J. Marzano. 1994. *The Systematic Identification and Articulation of Content Standards and Benchmarks.* Aurora, CO: Mid-Continent Regional Educational Laboratory.

Kruse, C. A. and G. D. Kruse. 1995. "The Master Schedule and Learning: Improving the Quality of Education," *NASSP Bulletin,* 79(571):1–8.

Leonhardt, M. 1993. *Parents Who Love Reading, Kids Who Don't.* New York: Crown Publishers.

Letteri, C. A. 1982. "Cognitive Profiles: Relationship to Achievement and Academics," in *Student Learning Styles and Brain Behavior: Programs, Instruments, Research.* Reston, VA: National Association of Secondary School Principals.

Letteri, C. A. 1985. "Teaching Students How to Learn," *Theory into Practice,* 14(2):112–122.

Letteri, C. A. 1988. "The NASSP Learning Style Profile and Cognitive Processing," in *Profiling and Utilizing Learning Style,* J. W. Keefe, ed., Reston, VA: National Association of Secondary School Principals.

Littleton High School. 1993. *Graduation Requirements and Demonstrations: Classes of 1995–96.* Littleton, CO: Littleton Public Schools.

Maeroff, G. I. 1993. "The Assault on the Carnegie Unit," *Education Week,* 13(6): October 13, 1993.

Mahaffey, R. 1993. "McDonald's USA CEO Discusses Education, Students, and Change: An Interview with Edward Rensi," *The High School Magazine,* 1(2):25–27.

Mahaffey, R., ed. 1995. *The Bulletin,* 79(571):issue. Includes Kruse, C. A. and G. D. Kruse. "The Master Schedule and Learning: Improving the Quality of Education"; Buckman, D. C., B. B. King and S. Ryan. "Block Scheduling: A Means to Improve Climate"; Huff, A. L. "Flexible Block Scheduling: It Works for Us!"; Edwards, C. E., Jr., "Virginia's 4 × 4 High Schools: High School, College and More"; Boarman, G. L. and B. S. Kirkpatrick. "The Hybrid Schedule: Scheduling to the Curriculum"; Shortt, T. L. and Y. Thayer. "What Can We Expect To See in the Next Generation of Block Scheduling?"; and Wilson, C. "The 4:4 Block System: A Workable Alternative."

Marshall, R. and M. Tucker. 1992. *Thinking for a Living.* New York: Basic Books.

McCarthy, B. 1981. *The 4-Mat System: Teaching to Learning Styles with Right/Left Mode Techniques.* Barrington, IL: Excel Corporation.

McLuhan, M. 1964. *Understanding Media.* New York: McGraw-Hill.

McLuhan, M. and Q. Fiore. 1968. *War and Peace in the Global Village.* New York: Bantam Books.

Miller, R. I. 1967. *The Nongraded School: Analysis and Study.* New York: Harper & Row Publishers.

National Commission for the Principalship. 1990. *Preparing for Our Changing Schools.* Fairfax, Virginia.

Presseisen, B. Z., R. J. Sternberg, K. W. Fischer, C. C. Knight and R. Fuerstein. 1990. *Learning and Thinking Styles: Classroom Interaction.* Washington, DC: National Education Association and Research for Better Schools.

Reinert, H. 1976. "One Picture Is Worth a Thousand Words," *The Modern Language Journal,* 60(4):160–168.

Rider, R. 1994. "Hayes High School, Delaware, Ohio," *The High School Magazine,* 2(2):20–21.

Robertson, R. 1994. "The Richmond County Program," *The High School Magazine,* 2(2):25.

Sizer, T. R. 1992. *Horace's School.* Boston: Houghton-Mifflin Company.

Stacy, M. 1994. "Gainesville History? They Wrote the Book," *Gainesville Sun,* Gainesville, FL, June 1, 1994.

Tanner, D. 1994. "A Nation Truly at Risk," *Phi Delta Kappan,* 75(4):288–297.

The Secretary's Commission on Achieving Necessary Skills. 1991. *What Work Requires of Schools: A SCANS Report for America 2000,* Washington, DC: U.S. Department of Labor.

Thomas Haney Secondary Centre, Maple Ridge-Pitt Meadows School District, Maple Ridge, British Columbia.

Traverso, H. 1995. *New Directions in Scheduling the Secondary School, 2nd ed.* Reston, VA: NASSP.

Trump, J. L. 1974. "DPIE, S-R, and Memory," *NASSP Bulletin,* 58(382):119–125.

Trump, J. L. 1977. "Are Counselors Meeting Students and Teacher Needs?" *NASSP Bulletin,* 61(410):26–28.

United Way of America. 1988. *The Future World of Work: Looking toward the Year 2000.* Alexandria, VA: United Way of America.

Wittrock, M., ed. 1980. *The Brain and Psychology.* New York: Academic Press.

Woodburn, J. H. 1972. *General Science.* Irving, TX: The Boy Scouts of America.

THROUGHOUT HIS THIRTY-NINE years in professional education Dr. John M. Jenkins has held directorships and administrative positions. He has also taught at the elementary, middle, high school levels and at the university level.

After five years as principal of Miami Springs High School in Dade County, Florida, Dr. Jenkins accepted the position of associate professor of education at the University of Miami, Coral Gables. He taught graduate courses in curriculum, instruction and administration. In 1971 he was appointed principal of Wilde Lake High School in the new city of Columbia, Maryland. Following eight years of service at Wilde Lake High School, he accepted the position of Director of Secondary Education for Lee County, Florida. After four years with Lee County, Dr. Jenkins became director of the P. K. Yonge Developmental Research School on the campus of the University of Florida, Gainesville, a position he held for twelve years. Currently, he is retired as a professor of educational leadership in the College of Education, University of Florida.

In 1963 he was selected as one of the first administrative interns nationally for a special training program involving the Ford Foundation and the National Association of Secondary School Principals (NASSP). He was assigned to the first nongraded high school in the United States at Melbourne, Florida. Dr. Jenkins represented the United States at an international conference on the changing role of the teacher in 1967. While principal of Wilde Lake the school was selected as one of 32 schools in the Model Schools Project sponsored by the Danforth Foundation and NASSP. In 1975 he was selected by the

Rockefeller Foundation as one of the sixty most effective high school principals in the United States. The *Executive Educator* magazine named him one of the top 100 educational executives in North America in 1987.

He served as a member of the Governor's Commission for the Improvement of Secondary Education in Florida in 1982. He worked for six years as a special consultant to the Florida Department of Education for the Teachers-as-Advisors program beginning in 1984. In that capacity, he provided technical assistance to over 200 middle and high schools and produced an annual evaluation of the project. He is an adviser to the Carnegie/NASSP Commission on the Restructuring of the American High School.

He has served as a site visitor for the U.S. Department of Education's National Secondary School Recognition Program and as an evaluator of grants for the same department. He chairs five and ten year evaluations of high schools for the Southern Association of Colleges and Schools.

Dr. Jenkins received his B.A. degree in 1955, his M.A. in 1961 and his Ed.D. degree in 1967 from the University of Miami, Coral Gables. He has completed additional work in educational research at the University of Wisconsin, Madison.

He has co-edited four books: (1) *Curriculum Development in Non-graded Schools* (1969), (2) *The Instructional Leadership Handbook* (1987, 1990), (3) *Restructuring for an Interdisciplinary Curriculum* (1992) and (4) *World Class Schools: An Evolving Concept* (1994). He co-authored *Developing Cognitive Skills* (1990) to accompany the NASSP *Learning Style Profile*. He is the author of *Advisement Programs: A New Look at an Old Practice* (1992). Additionally, he has written numerous articles on subjects such as leadership, change, learning styles, school discipline and advisement. Dr. Jenkins is department chair for instruction for the *International Journal of Educational Reform* where he writes a quarterly article.

He is married, has three children, two sons and a daughter. For fun he runs marathons and other distance races.